GET ME TO
— ZERO —

*How and why, it makes sense for middle
class Americans to retire debt free,
income tax free, and risk free.*

By Philip C. Gallant

Copyright © 2023 by Philip C. Gallant

Get Me to Zero
How and why, it makes sense for middle class Americans to retire debt free, income tax free, and risk free.

Forward by: Barry James Dyke
Author of *The Pirates of Manhattan*

To Contact Phil:
phil@theoptimusgroupllc.com;
info@theoptimusgroupllc.com,
518-688-9006
1-800-517-1430

Paperback ISBN: 979-8-9856101-5-4
Hardback ISBN: 979-8-9856101-6-1

FIRST EDITION

Published in the United States
by J Remington Press.
www,jremingtonpress.com

GET ME TO
ZERO

"In the days ahead, we all need to get to ZERO. Zero debt. Zero Taxes. Zero risk. As you strengthen your personal balance sheet, and develop strategies for a successful retirement plan, you can get to ZERO.

Zero debt. Zero Taxes. Zero Risk. If you take Phil's advice to heart, you will become more independent, escape financial bondage, and open up opportunities when you Get to Zero."

- Barry James Dyke

Contents

Acknowledgments

I could never have completed this book without the help and encouragement of some pretty amazing people. Allow me to thank them.

Kent Merrell

Kent was indispensable in his assistance and guidance creating and publishing this book. Since this is my first, I had no idea what to expect. His help and knowledge were unbelievably helpful! Thanks so much Kent!

Richard Bufkin

When I discussed the book concept with my longtime friend Richard Bufkin, I got nothing but support. Thank you for everything Richard!

Barry James Dyke

Everyone needs a sounding board in this business and for many years, Barry has been that for me. His knowledge and support throughout the years has been invaluable.

Erin and Amy

If I did not have the world's best staff, I could not have taken the time it took to write this book. Many of our clients have told me over and over what a joy and pleasure it is to work with Erin Schmiedchen, and Amy Taylor, who are as big a part of the team as I am. I am beyond grateful for them!

Kevin Johnson

We all have times in our lives when we need a true friend. I had a huge need for such a friend as I left the corporate world in 1997. Kevin Johnson, CEO of Advisors Insurance Brokers of Clifton Park, New York was that friend I needed back then. Kevin was the truest friend anyone could ask for at that time in my life. Without his help, I'm not sure I would still be in this wonderful business.

Michelle Gallant

My wonderful wife Michelle was so supportive through the writing process. She is my reason to live joyfully each day!

My Awesome Clients

The gift of being in this business is the wonderful relationships you develop with the folks we work with. I have a life filled with amazing friends who started out as clients. You are all so very important and I am thankful for you every day!

I thank all my friends and colleagues in the industry who encouraged me to write this book and for whom I have immeasurable admiration.

To my late Mom and Dad. I love and miss you both every day. Thanks for raising me the right way and giving me opportunities.

Forword
By Barry James Dyke

Today, few advisors, and too few consumers understand the unbridled speculation occurring within their retirement savings plans. Regrettably the majority of the population has been bamboozled by the media, the government, Wall Street, and the asset management industrial complex that the value of their 401(k)s always go up.

Stock markets do not always go up. The truth is that attempts to predict, forecast, or model returns has confounded academics and mathematicians for decades. Take a brief look at Japan. The Nikkei 225 in Japan, which is similar to our S&P 500 index of stocks crashed in 1990 and was one of the most spectacular stock market collapses in history. Over the past 30 years the Nikkei in Japan has mostly gone backwards and has barely moved upward.

In the U.S and worldwide, 2022 was a bloodbath for retail savers in 401(k)s, mutual funds, and ETFs. The S&P 500 Index, the main barometer of stock market performance lost -22%. The Dow Jones Industrial Average, which consists of major industrial companies lost -9%, while the tech heavy NASDAQ lost -33%. For thirteen years the excessive money printing by the Federal Reserve pushed markets up. But now that party has come to an end. There is plenty of roadkill and collateral damage. Silicon Valley Bank, First Republic, Signature Bank and Silvergate Bank have collapsed and gone into receivership, causing tens of billions of losses to the FDIC, backed by the taxpayer. These banks were supposed to be at the vanguard of finance and wealth management, but in the end, they were some of the worst risk managers in U.S. economic history.

Like the South Sea Bubble or Holland's tulip craze, crypto

currencies were the latest financial mania and bubble. FTX/ Alameda, Celsius Network, Coin Cloud, CoinFLEX, Compute North Holdings, Digital Currency Group, Three Arrows Capital, Voyager Digital, all companies whose core business was crypto currencies are now in bankruptcy. Surviving companies in crypto currencies are hanging on by a thread. What confused the retirement saver even more was that major financial institutions such as Fidelity, UBS, Wells Fargo, PayPal, Morgan Stanley, MasterCard, Credit Suisse, Citigroup, Charles Schwab, BlackRock, Barclays, and others were all embracing crypto currencies in some major way.

Regrettably in world league tables, because of this excessive speculation, American's retirement systems resemble that of a third world country. In terms of retirement and savings preparedness, according to the Mercer Global Pension Index, in 2021 the U.S.A ranked #19 in the world's top twenty, sandwiched between Hong Kong and Uruguay who were #18 and #20 respectively. Worse still, in terms of financial integrity, the U.S. ranked dead last.

It is time to get off the crazy train of speculation, leave Disneyland and get serious about planning your financial future. Now more than ever you need a well-informed, honest, independent advisor and author who will guide you and help you prosper in the days ahead. You need someone who will help you preserve the assets you have, insulate you from the Wall Street casino and give you an inflation hedge.

Phil Gallant's new book, Get Me to Zero is sage advice for most Americans. In the days ahead, you need to strengthen your personal balance sheet, and develop proven strategies for a successful retirement plan. Phil is a man of integrity, compassion and intelligence who goes the extra mile to help educate his clients and fellow advisors.

In the days ahead, we all need to get to ZERO. Zero debt. Zero Taxes. Zero risk. As you strengthen your personal balance sheet, and develop strategies for a successful retirement plan, you can get to ZERO. Zero debt. Zero Taxes. Zero Risk. If you take Phil's advice to heart, you will become more independent, escape financial bondage, and open up opportunities when you Get to Zero.

After writing three best-selling books on finance and retirement planning, I am convinced that the best thing one can do is probably do the exact opposite of what banks, mutual funds and other giant asset managers frequently recommend.

As an advocate for the common man, Phil Gallant's Get Me to Zero is welcome sunlight to a financial industry that loves to keep their clients and prospects in the dark. Good luck and God bless.

Barry James Dyke
North Hampton, New Hampshire
www.barryjamesdyke.com
May 25, 2023

Robert Ritter   (1934 – 2022)

Dedication

Get Me to Zero is my first book. When thinking about dedicating a book, I always thought it would naturally need to be dedicated to someone I love, my wife, my parents, or a friend. When I thought about this book's dedication, it was quite simple.

In any profession, there is usually someone who has made a life-changing impact on the trajectory of your career. I've been blessed to meet and rub shoulders with some of the greatest people in the history of my profession. I've met countless men and women who I would describe as tutors or mentors. I have known some of the brightest minds in the industry like my friend Barry James Dyke who was kind enough to write the forward to this book.

When I considered this dedication, it was crystal clear to me that I wanted to dedicate this work to Robert Ritter, the inventor and teacher of the InsMark illustration System. I first learned about this System when I traveled to San Francisco for an InsMark conference in the early 2000's.   There I saw this distinguished gentleman working with one of the software's main programs now known as Wealthy and Wise, but back then it was called "InsGift."

What struck me was that I was watching someone demonstrate the concept of "Do it vs Don't Do it" regarding financial alternatives with software that helped to clarify very important financial decisions. I was immediately drawn to not only the mathematical nuances, but also to the fact that I no longer had to rely upon "selling skills" to help my clients make complicated financial decisions. Complicated financial decisions are often also tied to complicated life decisions. They are generally also part of how to help families and business owners plan to leave a financial legacy because they loved their family, their employees, their businesses.

I did not know Bob Ritter well. I spoke to him many times at InsMark conferences, and I was honored to be a main platform presenter a couple of times at these conferences where I learned more about financial planning than any other conference I attended throughout my career. Bob's software and his teaching on how to use it completely transformed my career and it was a main reason I felt confident to become a retirement income planner. But there's something more about Bob Ritter that calls me to dedicate this work to him.

I once read a book called, "The Retirement Myth" by a fellow named Craig Karpel. In it, I learned the many risks associated with retirement income planning and why retirement is still a relatively new concept in America. As few as three generations ago, there were no retirement safeguards and retirement was for the wealthy. Most Americans continued to work until shortly before they died. That is how life was not so long ago. Bob Ritter worked until his passing. He never "retired" from his passion for helping financial advisors like me to become more informed, more dedicated to the financial truth inside a family's finances, and more able to help people solve financial puzzles. My career would have been very different had I never met Bob Ritter. It was, I am sure, a divine intervention for me because this career has blessed me with countless clients who have become my friends over the years. I've learned that with the right tools to discuss financial decisions, it doesn't have to be a "sell job", it just must be understood. Bob's software has helped me with that most important task.

Thanks Bob, for my lifetime of using what you taught me to create a dream life of helping people plan for their financial future. Like you, I have no plans to retire, even though I help my clients to plan for that exact event! Like you, I hope to die in the saddle helping as many people as I can along the way. Thank you for all I learned from you. This book is dedicated to your memory with humility and gratitude.

Introduction

Imagine this. It's the first day of your retirement. You wake up feeling happy and free. You know that the chaos in the stock market will not impact you anymore. You know that Uncle Sam can't steal any more of your income, and you don't owe a dime to anyone because you are completely debt free! How would you feel?

What would it be like to know that you have insulated yourself from the three biggest threats to your retirement security: 1) risk in the market, 2) taxes, and 3) debt. You are at ZERO in all three. You have ZERO debt. You have ZERO risk in the market. You have income on which you owe ZERO taxes. How would you feel?

It is possible. It is even likely that a skilled financial advisor or coach as I prefer to be called can help you to achieve that perfect retirement. But it must start somewhere. I believe it starts when you learn how to hire a financial advisor or coach to whom you give the following measurable goal. Get Me to Zero.

Get Me to Zero debt, including my home. Get Me to Zero income taxes. Get Me to Zero risk in the market.

If you agree that this is a goal worth achieving, it's critical that you know how to find an advisor who agrees with you. It's even more important that that advisor knows exactly what to do next. It's also important that they understand that these are the primary financial goals that you are determined to achieve before you retire, and that they are both skilled and able to help you do so. These are goals that can have measurable benchmarks along the way, and which allow you to assess the help you are receiving to get there.

I know how to hire a plumber. You probably do too. I know plumbers in my community. I have friends who have hired various plumbers to solve a problem. There are lots of plumbers who advertise on local radio and television. Finding a plumber is not the problem. When I hire a plumber, it's usually because I have a very specific plumbing problem. I have a clogged pipe. I have a leaking pipe. I need a new pipe installed. In other words, I have a specific problem that I need to solve and I can give the plumber very specific directions on what I want done and what the measure of success will be. We negotiate a price and once the job is done, the water flows accordingly. If it doesn't, I know that the specific objective has not been met. Simple. The same holds true for so many of the professionals that we hire to help us navigate life.

What about hiring a financial advisor? I don't even like the word "advisor" but that's what people tend to call us. What are your criteria for hiring an advisor? I once had a prospective client show up at my office for his first meeting with me and his first question was, "what's your track record?" I ended the meeting in the next five minutes. I'm not a stock market magician and I know that.

I informed this person that, if you want help investing your money, that's what stock brokers do. They have track records. Ask them. But it is unlikely that the stockbroker is going to do anything other than help you invest your money. And that's okay because that's their number one job. If you are looking for an advisor, who can work with all your investment and insurance needs, you might not pick a stockbroker first.

What most stockbrokers, who may or may not act as retirement income advisors, often don't do, is discuss your lifestyle risk profile in terms of replacing your income for your spouse and children or your partner in life if you die or become permanently disabled. They rarely, if ever discuss long-term tax planning. In fact, most broker dealers are averse to their brokers providing any kind of tax advice whatsoever. As far as risk is concerned, they are correctly going to invest your money according to your risk tolerance profile. You might rely upon their expertise to help you grow your investment portfolio, but that's usually a separate discussion from the investments you may be making in your retirement plans at work. As we know, and as Barry Dyke points out in his forward, there are no guarantees. I once heard a successful broker say, "Never mistake a bull market for a brilliant broker. In a bull market, we're all brilliant!" And finally, I'm pretty certain that a stockbroker is not going to help you figure out how to get out of debt. Quite honestly, that's not their job and it's not what they're trained to do.

Let me share a little background. Until the Revenue Act of 1978, which introduced the 401(k) to the American public, most working Americans had no experience whatsoever in investing money in the stock market. When this act took hold and corporations realized that they could off-load the retirement income risk to their workers, the old fashion pension plan rapidly began to disappear. Along with the disappearance of the pension, so came the disappearance of worker loyalty to one company. We lost the 30 years and a gold watch mentality. And we did so very quickly.

As 401(k) plans became more and more popular, mutual fund companies began a frenzied strategy to implement 401(k) plans in as many companies as possible. They gave the plans funds with beautifully designed brochures and names like "Lifestyle Funds" or "Nest Egg Builder funds" and so forth. All the employees had to do was "put money in from every paycheck" and voila! A happy and secure retirement was assured! Not only that, but these new investment plans helped us with our taxes because we voluntarily "elected to defer" some of the income we earned today to be taxed later when we retired, because after all, in retirement, we would likely be in lower tax bracket!

We didn't understand that we were likely making a series of financial mistakes that would plague us until the day came when we began to wonder whether or not we had done the right thing. We lowered our tax liability when at the time we likely had the most deductions, such as children to claim as dependents, mortgage interest to deduct, and for quite some time we could claim interest deductions on loans other than our mortgage. In fact, we lowered our taxable incomes during periods of time when just having a family and a house would give us a greatly reduced tax liability to begin with! In other words, many of us saved on taxes at exactly the wrong time!

In addition to that, we gave up liquidity, use, and control of our money for use during our lifetimes that may have caused us to take on more debt than we would have, had we had access to those funds just to handle what life throws at us year after year. For some, limited liquidity was actually a good thing to prevent us from spending our retirement savings, but for many it hasn't worked out so well.

As we hauled our kids off to soccer and baseball practices, we bought cars, and trucks, maybe even boats or RVs, and increased our lifestyle to enjoy the fruits of our hard work. We upgraded our homes and the neighborhoods we chose to live in. Then our kids get smart, and we want to send them to college! We take on more debt, we stop saving for retirement. We sign parent-plus loans.

Unfortunately for most of us, we could not save for retirement and increase our lifestyle without getting a little help, or maybe too much help from our friend, the credit card. Ever ask your grandparents what their credit score was in the 50's? Right. There was no such thing back then, and for good reason. People tended to live within their means. They used sophisticated techniques like budget envelopes and Christmas clubs. They had savings accounts. They paid down their mortgages. When they retired, they had a home that was paid for, and no other debt. Their income was primarily social security and savings, and while it was probably lower than their income in their working years, their needs were smaller because all the bills were paid. And maybe they took a few shots in the stock market, but it was less likely that they needed to make huge gains. So, most of the time they bought and held individual stocks that were only taxed if and when they sold them. And by the way, it's unlikely that they had an IRA of any kind.

Today, the sad truth and the result for far too many of us is that we end up paying as high as 34% in monthly interest payments while at the same time investing in a 401(k) that struggles to consistently earn 7% on average. In other words, we end up going backwards.

As you read on, it is my hope that you will come to understand, or maybe be reminded of some simple financial concepts that have stood the test of time and are never outdated. In fact, while many things around us are constantly changing, it is comforting to realize that we can go back to the future so to speak, armed with time tested strategies. If we knew these strategies before, we may have forgotten them. If you've never heard of them, it is high time you do!

Chapter One

The Land of Competing and Compounding Variables

I love vacations. Before the pandemic, my wife Michelle and I were constantly looking for vacations to go on. Michelle is retired now, but when she was a nurse mid-wife, we would go to many medical conferences where she could satisfy her continuing education requirements and I would happily tag along. We would get special conference rates for days before and after the conferences and we got to stay in beautiful hotels and resorts while on a partially tax-deductible business trip. We were truly blessed to have gone on some of the most amazing trips, mostly all due to Michelle's medical career. We were also extremely lucky that just about every trip went off as planned. We had no major flight delays or cancellations. We never lost our luggage. We didn't get sick or hurt while away. It could have been way different! Here's the point.

While we got great discounts on the rooms, we had to pay for them, plus the flights, and we always extended our stays to take advantage of the venues. Here's another little secret. We really couldn't afford it. We were both recovering from a divorce and our finances were a bit shaky. No, quite a bit shaky. But we went anyway. We wanted to create those memories together while we were as young as we were going to be together and we managed to pay them off quickly, but honestly the more financially responsible thing to do would have been to save the money, pay off some debt. We went on the trips, and we'll never regret it! I bet you've made a similar decision once or twice, and like me, you don't regret it. If you're wondering how we paid for it, it was a combination of Michelle's saving up for the flights and hotels and yes, using credit for the rest of it. I'm a huge believer in the fact that it's really important to live life now, every day. That belief however can quickly get you behind the eight ball financially if you're not careful. These trips went smoothly for us, but things could have gone very differently.

Imagine a long-planned trip from upstate New York where I live, to Cabo San Lucas Mexico. It's the middle of February and freezing at home and more than anything you're excited about the coming days of fun in the sun in Cabo. You're scheduled to fly out on Friday and as you watch the weather forecast on Tuesday evening, you see that there's a nor'easter heading up the east coast and the expectation is that your departure airport is going to be in the middle of the storm. A Nor'easter in February usually means snow measured in feet. It's basically a winter hurricane. This is concerning since you booked your flight with frequent flyer miles. Not so easy to reschedule free flights, right? Two important variables have popped up for your planned trip. Should you try to re-book the trip now or wait out the storm and hope your airport is not impacted. It sure would be easy if you could just stick with your original flight plan. So, the weather and your booking method are now competing variables.

You decide, heck, we'll try to leave a day early. The problem is that you can't go directly to Cabo because they have no rooms in the hotel before your scheduled arrival. You check around and find a room at another hotel in Cabo, but the cost is outrageously expensive because it's peak season and you're only coming for one night. Now you have a third variable to consider. Leave early, get to a more expensive hotel for one night, and then switch to your own hotel the next day, or stick with the plan and keep your fingers crossed. The variables are starting to compete. You want to get there, and you're not sure if you should leave early or hope for the best on your original plan.

Once you're aware of the forecast, you're smart enough to know that your trip could quickly become a nightmare. You try to work out different solutions, but each new possibility creates another competing possibility. You consider trying to switch the flights. Should you get a room booked first? What if you switch the flights and there's nowhere to stay? If you book the room first and you can't switch the flights, you've booked a room for nothing. Now I don't want to beat you over the head with this analogy, but in some form, somehow, we've all been in a similar set of circumstances. We think things are going to go one way if we do what we're supposed to do, and then something happens, and we've got competing and compounding variables happening all over the place. Can you see how this kind of stuff happens in everyday life?

Many of our financial decisions in life have multiple competing and compounding variables. It's how and why many of us get into debt, get behind on planning for retirement, don't have a specific goal for our finances, and have trouble making financial decisions. Think about your financial life and all the competing and compounding variables you face every day, every year, and for the rest of your life. For example.

You get married and move into a small apartment and life is bliss. It's so much bliss, that soon you're expecting little miss bliss. Hmm, a variable has been introduced for sure! Now you need a larger apartment or maybe a starter home. The problem is that one of you is still in school and not contributing to the household income. Therefore, it's going to be much harder to upgrade to a bigger living environment, whether a first house or bigger apartment on one income. Now, you consider maybe finishing your degree later and going back to work, or maybe your spouse gets a second job. After sitting down and analyzing things your spouse decides to stop contributing to his retirement plan so that the take home pay will be higher. The only problem with that is he's pretty good with math. He understands that to save successfully one of the most important things to have is time. He does the math and realizes that if he stops his contributions for even just 5 years, the lost opportunity cost of that decision, (the lost contributions plus the lost earnings on those contributions) is hundreds of thousands of dollars at retirement. Now you realize you've got another competing and compounding variable, and life's just getting underway!

One of my very favorite books about money is *The Psychology of Money* by Morgan Housel. I strongly recommend that you read that book; next of course. The first chapter of his book made so much sense to me. The title of the chapter is "No One's Crazy." Housel is a brilliant and accomplished guy. His book is not something you'd expect from a former columnist for the Wall Street Journal. The basic thesis in chapter one is that no one's crazy because of the way they spend money, the things they believe about money, or the results they achieve with money. It's human experience with money that drives human financial behavior. What we learn about money and what we think we know about money are vastly different than simply knowing how to invest, or where to park your cash. Housel makes the point that our experience with money has the tiniest minuscule impact on the world, but 80% of the influence on us and our decisions surrounding money. Our beliefs and thoughts about money are another compounding variable. Let me share a personal example.

I grew up in a lower middle-class family in the textile mill city of Woonsocket, Rhode Island. This was a city heavily influenced by French Canadian people who either worked the first, second, or third shift at one of several huge textile mills in the city. At public places, restaurants and social gatherings in my youth, French was the language that was spoken. There was a huge migration of French Canadians in the mid to late 19th century in many cities and towns in New England most of which were textile producing. In fact, the industrial revolution is said to have started at Slater Mill in Pawtucket, Rhode Island, not 20 miles from where I lived. Many of these cities and towns were prime examples of the great American melting pot. We had many Italians in our city as well, including our neighbors the Casellis', Andrionis' and Canastraris'.

There was the upscale part of town where the mill owners lived. There were also for many years in the late 19th and early 20th century in Woonsocket, tenement houses in the "flat lands". There, rows of tenements, owned by the mill owners of course, housed many of these shift worker families. While my family did not work in the textile mills, we were part of that working class environment, and we lived in a town that had very clearly defined ideas about who was successful and who wasn't. The mill owners paid their shift workers who then paid rent right back to their employers. You guessed it, the mill owners owned many of the small food stores in town too.

Without getting into my family history and the reasons for our lot in life, let me just say that my family scrapped by, paycheck to paycheck. We lived in a small ranch house, and I thought we were living large. As a kid, I knew my parents struggled, but I never realized to what degree. I think about what they learned from their parents about money. It formed the messages about money that I remember. It went something like this. "Successful people are greedy and evil." "They own everything, and we just live to support them." "He just was lucky; his father gave him everything".

Success then I concluded, must only be for bad or lucky people. As a result, I developed a huge fear of success that has impacted me for my entire life. In my mind, I wondered why there was such a degree of difference between people who were successful and those who were content to just work in the mill and go home and enjoy their family. I admired them both actually. The simple life that many of the locals seemed content with and actually grateful for, and the grander, more luxurious and prestigious lifestyle of the successful crowd. Somehow, I've always felt stuck in the middle. But I'm not crazy. That was Housel's observation. And surely, no matter what you believe about money neither are you. It's important that you really know that. It will make a huge difference in how you make financial decisions in the future.

As you can see, all of these stories have competing and compounding variables. When it comes to your money however, getting clarity around your financial goals with specificity is going to serve you well. You do NOT need a financial "advisor" for that. You and your spouse need a yellow pad and some time to think about priorities. This book is really to help you understand what my long business life in the financial advisor industry has taught me to be the most important thing that I can do for my clients. My job is to help you to learn how to manage the competing and compounding variables in your life. I need to find out if you're a contented mill worker, and there's nothing wrong at all with that, or that you want to own the mill. Nothing wrong with that either! I propose that planning to get to ZERO can help to facilitate your dream, no matter which one it is. I want you to understand that in my opinion, the most important instruction you can give to any financial advisor, is to get you to ZERO. Zero Debt. Zero Taxes. Zero Risk. You will see as you read why Zero is actually the most powerful and liberating number in finance.

We are influenced by what we're taught about money and eventually by our experiences with money. Our personalities are involved in every decision we make surrounding money. When we begin a new life with a spouse or partner, and it involves co-mingling for finances, things can get complicated very quickly. When you add in competing ideas and compounding variables presented by life, it's no wonder that many American families are living on a treadmill, many times financed by debt. It's not intentional and it's not uncommon. And, like Morgan Housel, I too believe it's not because you're crazy.

This is why it is so important that some very distinct and clear financial goals are established as early as you become aware of the need to do so. It would make sense to have a direct conversation with your spouse or partner about your financial objectives. That is very often easier said than done. Consider the benefits of setting the goal of getting to ZERO as quickly as possible, or as close to Zero as you can in retirement. It all begins with an assessment of your debt and dealing with that issue first. Getting completely out of debt as soon as possible is a worthwhile financial goal that can be clearly defined, along with a specific date as to when you will accomplish it.

Chapter Two

Debt, an Attractive Life Partner, Until It Isn't.

Society expects you to live in debt. Want proof? Watch the next car commercial. They don't sell the MSRP, they sell the monthly payment. Zero down, zero interest and zero payments until next... whatever! This is NOT the get me to Zero plan I'm talking about in this book! But man, it's so attractive. Look at what they're selling!

Wouldn't you look fabulous in that new sports car? Wouldn't it be great to take your family to that island in the Caribbean where "everything's gonna be alright?" Doesn't it make sense to buy that RV now so your family can go camping, maybe even "glamping?" Isn't that in-ground swimming pool just what you need this summer? Yes! Yes, it is! And why shouldn't you and your family be rewarded for working hard? As I said in the last chapter, like my friend Morgan Housel, I too believe, you're not crazy. But more than likely if you buy into these messages, you're in debt. And you're like millions of other Americans in the same boat. In fact, as I write this, according to an article in "The Hill" on January 21, 2023 (1), the average US household is carrying $7,486 in credit card debt month to month and more than 14 million Americans have credit card debt of more than $10,000. Houston, we have a problem!

The other side of that coin is that Americans have driven economic growth in the United States by our willingness to stretch ourselves financially to enjoy the life we believe we deserve. Our appetite for the good life has stretched us into living on debt for huge homes, fancy cars, and luxurious lifestyles. We've made the economy run like crazy! As a society, and you might not like hearing this, we spend money we don't have, to buy things we don't need, to impress people we don't know. And while I believe you're not crazy,

I do believe that unless clearing yourself from debt becomes your very first financial priority, you will never truly achieve financial freedom. Hoping that you clear it up before you retire is not a plan. Hope is hope, it's not a financial strategy. Having a very specific plan and strategy to be debt free by a specific date is the first step to getting control over your financial life. Yet, it is the thing that we are likely to hide from our friends, our family, and even our spouse. Spending money is for many people a little hit of dopamine. We want what we want, when we want it. Period.

Why is this? I believe that we have multiple compounding variable reasons for the state of our financial affairs as a nation. I earnestly believe that the main culprit of our sick financial situation is the total lack of financial education from somewhere, anywhere! Even our politicians are devoid of understanding the basic tenant that spending money you don't have is poison for our economy!

As I pointed out in chapter one, our best financial education might not always come from our home environment. Our public and even private education resources do almost nothing to teach us how to deal with money. If you came of age in the 80's and 90's, you may understand what things were like just before then. I don't remember my parents owning a credit card when I was young. Thank God! My mom appeared to be conservative with money and my dad would buy anything once he got a credit card later in life. Turns out, they were both better spenders than they were savers. It's a sad commentary that my dad died with $7,000 in credit card debt, and $7,000 in an IRA. That was it. There was no debate about lifestyle management when I was young. You only got to spend what you earned. The only forms of credit I remember as a kid were lay away plans at the department stores. And guess what? You didn't get the merchandise until you paid off the lay away! But once credit became easier and easier to obtain, everything changed.

Whether you understand the thesis or not, and at the risk of becoming a little too technical here, I want to point out that we have undergone a collective shift from Austrian Economic principles, practiced by our parents, albeit unknowingly, but even more likely by our grandparent's generation, to a Keynesian economic model in our personal financial lives. What's the difference? The difference is like the distance between the moon and the stars.

Austrian economics is basically explained this way. A true economy should operate on a limited supply of money. There is no way to increase the supply of money, but it is critical that money have velocity in the economy. In other words, it needs to circulate. The circulation of money is what drives the economy. It's not called Austrian economics because that's how they do it in Austria, it's because many economists who believe in this theory happen to be Austrian. There's boatloads of books and articles on this. I love a book by Carlos Lara and Robert Murphy, PhD entitled, *"How Privatized Banking Really Works."*

Think of it this way.

Let's assume that the total supply of money in the United States is $1 Billion. What would you likely pay for a house based upon how much of that $1 billion pie was allocated to you for the work you did, and the income you earned. If you earned $100,000, you would be one of only 10,000 people in total who could earn that much in a $1 billion economy. Since as of this writing there are approximately 350 million people in the United States, you and 9,999 others would likely NOT make $100,000, but something much less. Obviously, that $100,000 would be an excessively high percentage of the total $1 billion in circulation. So, it's likely that your salary would be much smaller and reflective of your share of a much smaller pie, but so would the price of your home. Everything would have much lower costs. It wouldn't be cheaper, but it would be proportional based upon the total amount of available money. Austrian economics would have a major impact on the economic health of the country, let alone the world. A limited and countable money supply would mark assets to their true value. There would be hard assets backing every dollar. It's likely that if you needed a loan for that home, interest rates would reflect two things; one, that the value of the money being loaned was extreme and the interest rate would reflect that; and two, the ability to get that loan would be based upon real economic principles. It would be unlikely that banks or other institutions would be lending money haphazardly to just anyone on a whim. Remember so called "liar loans" during the 2008 housing crisis? Credit checks would be more extensive, loan terms would be very specific, and yes, most loans in an Austrian model would need to be fully collateralized. There could not be such a thing as a credit card. Money would have tremendous value in an Austrian economy.

But that's not how we operate our global economy. Our global economy operates on a Keynesian model where fiat money is all the rage. What is fiat money? Well, I guess the best example is how on May 4, 1626, Peter Minuit purchased the Island of Manhattan for $24 worth of buttons and cloth from the Native American tribe called the Canarsee. (Turns out it wasn't such a bad deal for the Canarsee since they didn't own the island in the first place!). In other words, fiat money is what is declared to be money. Our American dollar is only worth anything because our government dictates by fiat that it is, and as of this writing, the world still believes that.

I know I'm not alone in wondering where this money comes from and how we're ever going to pay it back. I have the first answer. It comes out of the sky. It's created out of thin air. Therefore, what do you think it's real worth is? Correct. Not much. And THAT'S why houses don't cost $12,000 like they would in an Austrian model, they cost several hundred thousand dollars. That's why we had a 2008 crisis when banks were approving so called "liar loans" and giving mortgages to people who had no business qualifying for a loan of several hundred thousand dollars. That's what created mortgage-backed securities. That's why creating those securities lead to creating even riskier mortgage-backed securities, and that's why we had credit default swaps. It's also the reason why the price of everything has gone through the roof! It's not because things are more expensive, it's because our money loses value every time, we print another Trillion.

The argument is that all of this money, especially since we went off the gold standard in the early 70's, has created a booming economy in housing, the auto industry, the luxury vacation industry, the .... industry. The list goes on and on. It's all beautiful glitter and gold, but the truth is, it's not worth what it's worth if we collectively decide it isn't. We feed the beast with our consumer mentality, and we are just playing our part. But remember what I said in Chapter one. Like my friend Morgan, you STILL aren't crazy.

So, the real question is when are YOU going to take charge of your personal economy? We know that we can afford certain things, and other things are out of reach. It gets more out of reach every time we rack up more debt whether it be on a credit card or a loan for a new truck. Unlike the government, which can simply print more paper and call it money, we must rely upon what our income can handle. If you think about it, whether we like it or not, we must operate our households with an Austrian mentality, even though we can "buy stuff" we don't have the money for like a true Keynesian! If we operate the same way the government does, eventually, our payments will exceed our income and when that happens, it's time for an appointment with a bankruptcy attorney. The party's over. We can't print any more money. The Government can. So, I guess we shouldn't follow the government's lead.

This discussion leads us to having to answer one huge question. Do we want to live an Austrian styled financial life, or a Keynesian style when we're retired. If your answer is that you like the Austrian model, then it's clear that you want your own economy, and your own ability to operate in this crazy economic environment. If that is true, then the very first thing you must do is figure out how to get to ZERO debt as soon as possible. The question is how.

If you do just the most basic search about getting out of debt, you will find all kinds of debt relief, debt consolidation, debt elimination programs out there. Most of these can help you with debt in some form or fashion, but they won't change your personal economic behavior and they won't lead you down a solid road to creating your own personal economy. If you're a fan of Dave Ramsey, you know that he says that all resources need to be applied to paying off your debt. The problem is, following Dave's rules, you're paying off debt, but you're not creating an asset that can help you not only to stay out of debt to banks and credit card companies but can also set you on the road to creating a powerful financial asset that will become the basis for your personal Austrian economic model.

I am tempted here to go through an exhaustive recitation of what to do and how to do it. As I thought about writing this book, I realized that my number one job was to help you to understand that the most important number in your financial life is zero.

There are many ways to create a plan to rid yourself of debt. You can follow a system like the one used by Dave Ramsay which essentially is a plan to dramatically change your lifestyle and redirect every extra penny to eliminating your debt. Clearly, thousands of people have successfully changed their lives by doing just that. But is that the only way?

The real goal in my mind in addition to eliminating debt is to gain the financial confidence that comes with knowing you are out from under the debt cycle, and now have a measure of personal economic strength. I use that term intentionally. It's one thing to say you have economic wealth, a healthy balance sheet if you will. It's another to know that you have personal economic strength. Personal economic strength is when you are finally free of the burden of debt from banks and other financial institutions and can personally finance anything you want through your own self-created personal economy. Having the knowledge that you can negotiate a cash deal for most major purchases once you've established yourself in this position, and being able to self-finance them in the future, without leaving your loved ones in debt after you're gone, gives you tremendous financial confidence and power.

The question is, what kind of debt elimination program will contribute to your gaining personal economic strength through the elimination of all your debt, including your home? I am aware of several programs that not only help you to eliminate your debt but do so in a way that creates a highly valuable financial asset that can play a huge role in achieving the other two Get Me to Zero goals of zero income taxes, as well as zero risk on your draw-down assets. I will elaborate on this in the next chapter. For now, however, imagine that you achieve the goal of having ZERO debt several years before you retire. Imagine also that you will be able to never have to use traditional banking ever again when you're retired. Imagine the powerful feeling you will have. This is an important and solid financial goal. It is measurable. A timeline for its completion can be established and followed.

That's why the first charge to your financial advisor in the Get Me to Zero challenge is, get me to ZERO debt. Once you achieve that goal, everything changes.

Chapter Three

One Step Closer to Freetirement!

It is my belief that all of us fundamentally want one thing: freedom!

While many of us know the term, we probably can't whistle the tune to the famous song by Johnny Paycheck, *"Take This Job and Shove It!"* If you've never felt that way about your job, consider yourself lucky. Many Americans work in jobs they would never do if they didn't need the money. In fact, one of the most interesting things I observed after the Covid 19 Pandemic and the associated lock downs and lock outs, was how hard it was to get people to come back to work in an actual work environment.

Many workers who could work from home decided that they liked the freedom of not having to commute to the office. They probably also liked not having to deal with that annoying mouth breather in the next cubicle. They didn't have to worry about parking, and lunch and, well, just a host of other stuff. Working from home gave them the feeling of independence. As I observed this, I couldn't help but think about how and why this really helped to make my point about what we truly want in life. As I said previously, it is my belief that all of us fundamentally want one thing: freedom. That freedom usually starts with financial freedom.

Imagine that you're working on your retirement plan, (whether or not you admit it, you are). As I mentioned in the previous chapter, you've worked with your advisor or financial coach and you've eliminated your debt, including your mortgage! Now, all the money that was going towards your mortgage is being saved at a ferocious rate in a strategy designed to help you build a plan to stay out of debt permanently. It is through the use of a financial tool where you're earning uninterrupted compound interest. Not only that, if you need access to the funds you have accumulated, you have a contractually guaranteed right to access them, either by withdrawing them, or by acting as your own banker and borrowing from yourself. That's right. Your debt elimination strategy included the strategic use of a time-tested financial tool that, once you have fully capitalized it, allows you to self-finance almost anything you want.

Why using Life Insurance as part of your debt elimination strategy is a savvy move.

As a veteran of the life insurance industry for these many years, I find it amazing that many so called financial "gurus," who while extremely popular in the media, protect themselves by calling their advice, "financial entertainment." Their radio show advice is often nothing more than a hard and fast opinion, and they often dismiss permanent life insurance as a powerful financial tool out of hand. I'm talking about national media financial heroes who demonstrate an overwhelming ignorance of not only how different types of life insurance policies actually work, but who also make it more likely that someone without this knowledge is probably going to run their finances like a Keynesian! Preaching a lifestyle reduction strategy as the best way to get out of debt might be popular, and it works if you do it, but it is not financial advice so much as it is lifestyle management. Get Me to Zero is an economic concept, not a product. The Get Me to Zero concept is a way for you and your advisor or financial coach to measure three vitally important goals throughout your life. In chapter one, I used the concept of compounding variables to illustrate that finding yourself in an uncomfortable amount of debt is likely something that sneaks up on you and before you know it, you have a financial issue that makes you more than a little uncomfortable. It's about a lack of knowledge, not a lack of character or self-discipline. Never allow yourself to be shamed into doing something at the expense of something else that may serve you better. Sometimes, all it takes for a better outcome is a little more knowledge.

What are the advantages of incorporating a whole life insurance contract into your strategy? Let's start with some basics.

First: Once you are working on the insurance side of the fence with your money, you are now working under contract law. Insurance policies, for the most part, are unilateral contracts. A unilateral contract is one where one party has one obligation, (for the policy owner, that's usually premium payments) and the other party (the insurance company) must honor all the terms and conditions laid out in the contract. That's why when you purchase an insurance contract you can know what the expectations are, by contract.

Second: In most states, life insurance cash values carry special asset protection features, such as protection from predators and creditors. That means that in the event of a lawsuit or even a credit crisis, life insurance cash values may have protection from both. Amounts vary from state to state, but this is why many professionals like physicians, and construction company owners tend to have a huge amount of cash value life insurance. Many times, they purchase these policies purely for the asset-protection feature alone!

Third: For your grandparents, whole life insurance policies were one of the safest places they had access to as a savings vehicle. Since there were very few savings alternatives prior to the Employee Retirement Income Security Act (ERISA), banks and life insurance companies were the primary source of savings for those Americans who chose to save. Specifically, whole life insurance has a special place in the financial strategies of not only the average American family, but also for the wealthy. Many wealthy families understood and continue to understand that the special tax treatment, safe accumulation features, and dividend potential from whole life insurance was and still is an integral part of building family and generational wealth. To be clear, life insurance is insurance first but is also an important and extremely powerful savings vehicle second. It is NOT an investment however, and it should never be compared to investing. Investing and finance are different.

Besides your grandparents and the wealthy having a good understanding of the value of whole life insurance, there is another key player in the financial world that holds life insurance in the highest regard: banks. Large banks have used life insurance cash values as an integral part of their tier-one capital for decades. It's through a program known as BOLI, (bank owned life insurance). This is where banks purchase cash value life insurance on their key executives and then use the cash values as part of their tier one (most conservative) capital reserves. For many large banks, cash value life insurance is the largest asset on their balance sheet!

Four: Whole life insurance cash values have guaranteed growth. While we cannot compare the growth in these policies to the potential growth in the stock market over a long-time horizon; this is not the proper way to compare this asset with any other. This guaranteed growth is part of the pricing the life insurance companies use to make certain that their policies grow in value. Company actuaries do these calculations. (A friend once told me an actuary is an accountant without a personality!) Actuarial science is the method used to price these insurance products and manage the balance sheet. Yes, science. In addition to the guaranteed cash value growth, life insurance policies with mutual life insurance companies pay dividends. Dividends are important in that they enjoy special tax treatment. In fact, the word "dividend" comes from the life insurance industry. Here's how it works, in very simple terms.

A mutual life insurance company is owned by the policy owners and is not traded on any stock exchange. Most life insurance companies today, however, are stock companies. Their first obligation is not to their policy owners, it is to the stockholders. A Mutual company calculates all its revenues from all sources including but not limited to premium payments, policy loan interest, and investment income, and then subtracts operating expenses and claims paid, to come up with what we call a divisible surplus. They then distribute the surplus as a dividend to the owners of the company, who happen to be the policy owners. The United States tax code has also recognized an extremely important fact regarding dividends. Since mutual companies calculate the payable dividends each year, the dividend paid, represents a return of an overcharge of premiums. That's because the actuaries who price the life insurance policies overcharge the premiums needed over the lifetime of the policy in the early years. Therefore, life insurance dividends, with very few exceptions, can be withdrawn tax free!

Finally, life insurance has a self-completing component. For example, if Mr. Jones is maxing out his 401(k) contribution each year and has accumulated, let's say $100,000 in his account and then dies, Mrs. Jones is left with a taxable asset. Since 401(k) money is subject to market fluctuations, maybe at death, the account is worth less than the amount invested, and it's taxable to boot! Saving money in a life insurance account is a self-completing strategy. That's because if Mr. Jones dies prematurely, the death benefit, which is ALWAYS higher than the amount paid, is completely tax free to Mrs. Jones as a survivor. There is no more efficient way in the world to distribute wealth.

So, knowing all of this, how does a Specially Designed Insurance Contract help you become "Freetired"?

Once you have executed the first part of your plan, which is to become completely debt-free, including your home, think about your cost of living at that point. You won't need money for "payments" on anything except perhaps your property taxes if you own a home. You won't need to worry about being homeless if the economic sky falls, since with most debt elimination plans, which include a whole life policy, the clients end up with significant cash values in their policies. Once you have all your debt eliminated, you can then begin to save even more efficiently. Perhaps at that point, you will want to add a hybrid life insurance policy for cash accumulation. By hybrid, I mean a policy that allows you to participate in upside market performance, but not the downside. These policies, when structured properly, can be a critical component to their success by helping you accomplish the next two zero goals; zero taxes and zero risk. They become a fantastic addition to your Get Me to Zero (GMTZ) strategy! More on these policies later.

Chapter Four

The Cost of Tea, and All That

I grew up just about 50 miles south of where the Boston tea party took place. In the famous story of the events that led up to the American Revolution, we all learned about the night of December 16th, 1773, when about 60 American patriots disguised themselves as Mohawk Indians and threw 342 cases of tea from the East India Tea Company into Boston Harbor. You can read the details in a good American history book, but the bottom line was that the protesters were upset about two things; first that there was taxation without representation, and second that the British had made it impossible for any company except the East India Tea company to sell tea in the colonies. This made Samuel Adams, (who I personally believe was the major instigator of the revolution in the taverns and churches of Boston) and his Sons of Liberty very upset. Thus, on that fateful night, they literally disposed of a boat load of tea in protest of taxes, which lead to a bunch of farmers defeating the world's largest military force at the time! Talk about an aversion to taxes!

Our founding revolution was partly and largely based upon a reaction that taxes were (and I would argue today still are) in large part, unfair. The unfairness today in my view doesn't stem from the fact that we must pay income taxes, (although until congress passed the 16th amendment to the constitution on July 2, 1909 and ratified by the states in 1913, the Federal Government did not have the constitutional right to tax our income), but rather it comes from the fact that we have little or no say in how congress spends the money it raises from taxing our incomes. In short, I don't, and I suspect you don't, like the way the government spends our money. How many ridiculous items have you heard about over the years that

Congress has spent our money on? As an example, our government recently spent $442,340 to study the behavior of male prostitutes in Vietnam. It goes on and on. Most of us laugh about the ridiculous wasting of our hard-earned tax dollars. It's fun to laugh at, until it isn't. It's no fun to realize the tax mess we are in and why I believe strongly that it's about to get much worse.

I am going to propose a theory here. It's only my theory and I have no other sources to reference. This just comes from my thinking about and reading about how we've been duped into believing several financial theories that really benefit the government more than us. But first, let's see where we are tax wise and how we got here.

I read about the Studebaker Auto company pension problem a long time ago. If you've never heard the story, it is one that has had a huge impact on American workers ever since it happened. It is, in my opinion, one of the reasons we find ourselves in a retirement taxation hell hole today. The short story is that the Studebaker auto company closed its plant in December of 1963 in South Bend Indiana. Once they did so, they also terminated the pension plan for about 4,000 hourly wage employees. There is a fascinating paper about this published by James Wooten and the *Buffalo Law Review* entitled "The Most Glorious Story of Failure in the Business: The Studebaker-Packard Corporation and the Origins of ERISA."

ERISA is the Employee Retirement Income Security Act of 1974, which was signed into law on Labor Day, 1974 by President Gerald R. Ford. It was the culmination of the outcry caused by the failure of the Studebaker pension in 1963 that ultimately led to the creation of this legislation. There is a vast amount of historical data and lots to read about what I believe is the most consequential piece of legislation for Americans in the last 100 years. In my opinion, ERISA was the beginning of the end of corporate America thinking about the retirement welfare of its workforce. Essentially, ERISA required companies to fund their pension plans and report on their fiscal soundness on an annual basis. If you've ever left a job and needed to maintain your health insurance, COBRA (Consolidated Omnibus Budget Reconciliation Act) and HIPAA (Health Insurance Portability and Accountability Act) are part of the many revisions to ERISA.

What many of us do not realize however is that when ERISA

passed, corporations were already looking for a way out of being responsible for the retirement income security of their employees. If your parents or grandparents worked for a corporation with a pension, they were likely extremely loyal to that company because they wanted the security of a pension in retirement. Until recently, based upon Social Security formulas, the average Social Security check for most retired Americans was not enough to sustain a worker in retirement. It was really important therefore that pensions and savings were sufficient, and that Social Security served its intended function as a back stop and supplement for other retirement pensions and savings.

ERISA, is also the law that established the first Individual Retirement Accounts (IRAs). Back then, you were limited to a $1,500 annual IRA contribution, but only if you worked somewhere that did NOT offer a pension plan. My oh my, how things have changed.

The next big law to come around regarding retirement was the Revenue Act of 1978. This act was signed into law on November 6th, 1978, by President Jimmy Carter. The act established several new provisions to the tax code including the creation of Flexible Spending accounts. Among its more obscure provisions at the time was the inclusion of section 401(k) which was originally intended to limit executive compensation. It allowed for the establishment of "elective deferrals" which basically means that you decide on your own, to defer income which would otherwise be payable to you for work you did this year and take the deferred compensation in later years. It was the establishment of this provision that allowed corporations to get off the hook for retirement security for their employees. The 401(k) rapidly became the default pension plan in the United States. It created the rapid dissolution of old fashion pension plans now more rigorously overseen by the government under ERISA. It is also the beginning of the explosive growth in the stock market as it made average Americans investors in the stock market via the mutual funds in their 401(k) plans. Employers saved time and money by offloading the responsibility for retirement income security to its employees. Employees at the time thought the 401(k) gave them more flexibility to switch employers since they didn't have to stay with an employer they didn't like working for in order to qualify for a pension.

There is a load of problems with the 401(k)-retirement system.

Even though subsequent rules and regulations have attempted to fix some of these problems, the plan has some very serious limitations for the real world. Here are just a few of them.

1.   With few exceptions, the employee contributions are pre-tax "elective deferrals" of their income as we have seen. By electing to defer your income now, you don't pay taxes on income you earned this year until you begin taking funds from your 401(k) after you turn age 59 ½. Many people think this is a tax deduction. It is NOT a deduction; it is a deferral. In other words, there is no "write off" for your 401(k) contribution. Therefore, the impact on your taxes is the same as it would be if you worked at another job, but earned less take-home pay. Your taxable income, as well as your take home pay is reduced by the amount of money you defer to your 401(k) plan. Is that a good thing? It could be, but in many cases it's not so great once you retire and it's time to live on that money. You see, there's no guarantee on what tax bracket you will be in when you retire. I've had clients tell me they will be in a lower tax bracket when they retire thinking there's a special tax code for retired people. There isn't. In fact, by taking large sums of money from your 401(k) in retirement you could trigger the taxation of your Social Security benefits! That's correct. Social Security is only taxable once certain thresholds are exceeded from other income sources, like income from IRA and 401(k) plans! Even tax-free interest from Municipal Bonds counts towards your provisional income which is how the calculation of the taxes is done for Social Security. That's why saving in a tax deferred instrument like an Individual Retirement Account or IRA or a 401(k) plan is a great deal for the government! Imagine a business partnership where your partner doesn't tell you how much their share is until the business is established and has money! And imagine if that partner could change the deal at will! That's the partnership arrangement you have with Uncle Sam if you have the large majority of your retirement savings in tax deferred IRA and 401(k) plans.

2.   Liquidity, use, and control of your money during the savings years is severely restricted without subjecting yourself to penalties, and taxes. The 401(k) plan does not allow for the use of your retirement savings before retirement

with some very limited exceptions such as the purchase of a first home. While 401(k) plans offer loan provisions, they are limited and punitive to say the least. If you were the president of an investment firm, wouldn't it be awesome to have people buy into your mutual funds like clockwork, every time they got paid? Wow, what a deal! And, if those same investors had little to no clue about what they were buying, wouldn't that be even better? And what about if you could even penalize them for withdrawing their money earlier than retirement? That would be great too! Get the picture? You lose complete control of your retirement savings inside a 401(k) plan. I say that as my opinion. There are no laws that say you lose control, but in my mind, what control do you have? You might think that you can control what you invest in. Really? I would refer you to a couple of fantastic books about exactly what is going on with retirement plans and Wall Street by my good friend Barry James Dyke. Barry is the author of the forward to this book as well as a couple of must-read books on this topic, *The Pirates of Manhattan, 1 and 2*. Reading about what really goes on with Wall Street will turn your hair gray or whatever! The control over your money really lies with the institutional investors managing your plans funds, and according to Barry, it isn't pretty.

3.   Dollar cost averaging is the main method of saving in a 401(k). That means that you invest the same amount of money each pay period, but the number of shares you acquire is based upon the price of the shares that day or the next day. You see, while most of us think that investing is saving, it isn't. It's investing. When I am saving, my money contributions are not at risk of loss, and I earn interest on my saved money. Once I earn the interest, I don't lose it because of a change in the market. Investing on the other hand is the accumulation of fund shares. If the markets are going like gangbusters while I'm buying, it follows logically then that I am buying shares at a high price. It makes me feel good to be investing in a roaring market, but in reality, it's the opposite of almost every other purchase you have ever made! You want to buy low and sell high. That's why you've probably heard never to buy the most expensive house in the neighborhood. The best way to invest would be if the markets are sluggish and share prices are low while you're buying them. It just

makes sense that getting more for the same money is a great deal. Then, in retirement, when you want to take income from those shares by selling them as you need them, you want the share prices to climb as high as possible, so you only need to sell a few shares to obtain the income you need. If you purchased 20 shares of a fund at $5.00 per share when you're working with your $100 contribution, it would great if the share prices doubled by the time you needed to sell them. That way, you would only need to sell 10 shares to get the same $100, not 20. But who can guarantee that this is the way it's going to work out. No need to research the answer. The answer is no one.

4. If you were very focused on stuffing as much as possible into your 401(k) plan at the expense of any other form of savings, then you know that the government really has locked you out of accessing those funds without massive taxes and penalties before you reach age 59 ½. Life happens to us all in the meantime. There are countless things that come up in life for which we need to reach into our reserves. The 401(k) and IRA plans are so punitive that most of us try to avoid doing so at all costs. The truth is that the government is really anxious to get their hands on that money, but they, like you, want the pile to grow!

Back to my theory. I know that you might say I'm a conspiracy theorist for proposing this, and once again, it's only my opinion. Doesn't it make sense that the government gets into this 401(k) business, (albeit by accident since the original purpose of the 401(k) was for highly compensated employees to defer taxes due in the current year to the future) because they understood human behavior? Did they think that by acquiescing to the desire for the 401(k) to replace the traditional defined benefit plan that it would hurt them tax-wise? I think not. In fact, I believe that the early withdrawal penalties making it disadvantageous to use your retirement savings until AFTER you were 59½ helped Wall Street to salivate even more at the opportunity to make the average American an investor! If the government and Wall Street could collude, so to speak, and make that a normal part of the plan, then it follows that 401(k) balances would be higher. Higher balances mean more tax revenue.

You see, you make the salary deferral of let's say, $20,500 dollars when you're 45 years old. So, the government doesn't get to tax that $20,500 now. However, if you earn an average of 5% on that $20,500 for the next 20 years, it grows to over $66,000 by the time you turn 65. Do they only tax you on the original $20,500 you deferred? Heck no! They get to tax you on the entire $66,000! Plus, they don't even promise what the tax rate will be on that money. It's like starting a business partnership and your partner gets to decide after you've been successful how much his or her share of the partnership will be! Would YOU make that deal? In essence, when you stuff your 401(k), 403(b) for non-profits, or 457 plan for state and federal employees with cash, the government really hopes that you do extremely well! Why? TAX REVENUE BABY! That's right. I remember President Clinton projecting huge budget surpluses for many years in the future. The reason for this is that the stock market (built on dot com companies like Enron, Global Crossing, Pets.com, Webvan etc.) was booming in the 90's. But in 2000, the dot com bubble burst and the party was over. This had a HUGE psychological impact on millions and millions of Americans who were still new to the concept of being investors. People ran scared as the market was negative in 2000, 2001, 2002. Ironically, this is exactly when it was time to increase contributions! The surplus projection was predicated on millions of baby boomers hitting their peak earning years in the 90's and 2000's and the expected flood of money into their retirement plans that could be taxed later. The average investor got spooked and ether stopped contributing or reduced their contributions dramatically. This is only my theory, but I have a hunch I'm right. Of course, there are many other reasons why the 401(k) has limped along ever since, so much so that even Time Magazine has had at least two cover stories on why 401(k) plans are not so hot after all.

What are the Alternatives?

As an example, let's consider two brothers, we'll call them Tom and Carl, one of whom, Tom is investing in a 401(K) for 10 years While Carl is investing the same amount but has included life insurance in his plan. Let's assume that they are twins, both age 35. Where could they be 10 years later?

If Tom, the 401(k) guy is lucky, he's been investing in a down market and accumulating shares like crazy. After 10 years however, assuming Tom has been investing the maximum contribution of

$20,500 (as of 2023), and his employer has also contributed $6,000 per year, that's a total of $265,000 invested over the past 10 years. Assume his 401(k) statement at age 45, ten years later is $561,693. He has experienced a rate of return net of all fees of 4.07%. In order to do this however, and because he is so very worried about retirement, he has no significant additional savings. He has 20 years left on his 30-year mortgage and he has several "lifestyle" debts, such as two car payments, a boat payment, student loans for both he and his wife, as well as a home equity line of credit that is almost maxed out.

On the other hand, Carl puts $6,000 per year into his 401(k) plan and gets a 50% match from his employer on the first $6,000 so that a total of $9,000 goes into his 401(k) plan. At the end of his 10-year period, let's assume that he got the same return as his brother Tom, but the total investment has only been $90,000 and his balance has grown to $190,764. In addition, Carl has taken the remaining after-tax money that would have gone into the 401(k), or $11,600 (remember, he has to pay taxes on the difference) and he has purchased a whole life policy based upon that premium. This buys him a death benefit of about $425,000 and in 10 years he has an additional $106,000 in life insurance cash values. Carl has a total of $297,264 of cash and 401(k) savings combined and $450,000 payable tax-free to his spouse if he dies before retirement.

During the last 10 years, however, Tom has been making normal payments on his mortgage and his other bills, car payments, student loan debt, etc. Carl has been using his whole life insurance contract to eliminate all his debt. At the end of 10 years, Tom still has 20 years left on his mortgage, and Carl has paid his off. Not only has Carl paid off his mortgage, but he's also paid off all his other debts.

The question here is not who has more money, it is who is better prepared for what life is going to throw at him! If Tom dies, yes, his spouse, if he has one, does not have to take all the 401(k) money in a 10-year distribution term because she could roll it into her own or a spousal IRA. If she does that, it's not available to her until the she is 59 ½ without tax penalties and of course anything she would spend is subject to income tax as well.

If she rolls it into an inherited IRA to avoid the 10% penalty for early withdrawal, now she is subject to the 10-year distribution rule and must spend the inherited IRA within 10 years. Two not so great options!

If Carl dies, his wife can roll his 401(k) balance of $190,764 into her own IRA, and then immediately use tax-free proceeds from the life insurance policy to convert the entire IRA to a ROTH, thereby removing any income tax liability on that money for the rest of her life. That would take about $35,000 of the $425,000 tax-free death benefit leaving her with a Roth worth $190,764 and life insurance proceeds of $390,000. The life insurance proceeds are tax free, and she can use them any way she pleases. The only thing that is taxed on the remaining amount is interest on it if she puts it in the bank. Since the policy was being used to eliminate debt, depending upon when her husband dies, she may be close to being debt-free or may in fact already be there!

I am imagining a large swath of you saying, "she's better off with the higher 401(k)." While I admit that there's more money there, what is the point of it if she must pay taxes on all of the distributions? It does not provide liquidity until retirement unless she is willing to reduce it significantly by paying taxes and penalties if she takes money out before 59½. The real question is how much flexibility does Carl have vs Tom? More importantly, who do you think will have more financial or economic confidence during their working years?

While I have an opinion, you are entitled to yours as well. If you truly believe that it is better to put all your money into a 401(k), I understand, but keep reading, because the tax problems that can create might change your mind. But remember too, no one is crazy!

Chapter Five

You Can't Touch This...

In January 1990, a new MC Hammer song hit the charts called, "You Can't Touch This". I can hear it playing in your head right now! MC Hammer ended up losing a huge amount of money in the 90s, over 30 million dollars, by spending it poorly and employing over 200 people with a payroll of $1 million per month! Last I checked, he's now got a net worth of $2 million, and trust me, he probably says to everyone, "You can't touch this!"

With your money, wouldn't be great if it were in places where you could look old Uncle Sam in the face and tell him, "You can't touch this!" Well, there are only a few places to put your money where the law already says Uncle Sam can't touch this. We've discussed the importance of why you want ZERO debt, but what about Zero taxes? Well, here, I'm going to have to admit, you can't stop paying taxes altogether! Why? Because even if your income tax is zero, which is our goal, you still pay taxes just by being alive in America and functioning in society.

You get up in the morning and take a shower. Hmm, water tax. You wash yourself with soap you bought at the store, hmmm, sales tax. You drive to the store to buy something you need, hmmm sales tax. You need gas on the way home, hmmm, gasoline tax. You take your spouse to dinner, hmm sales tax. You stay home, hmmm property tax. It's easy to figure out that an unusually large portion of your income is already dedicated to paying taxes. The income taxes that you pay when you're retired, however, are mostly voluntary. Voluntary? Yup, voluntary!

You pay income taxes because the number one way that

Americans save for retirement is with tax-deferred vehicles like IRA accounts and 401(k) accounts and maybe even pension income, if you're lucky enough to have one. Each of these retirement financial tools is subject to income tax. That's bad enough news. But when you have a taxable retirement income, it also impacts the taxation of your Social Security income.

Taxation of Social Security

When President Franklin D. Roosevelt signed Social Security into law in 1935, he promised to never tax it. Maybe it's time to dig him up and make him keep that promise!

The way we've designed retirement systems here in the United States, taxation of Social Security benefits is here to stay. Roughly $35 billion dollars in income taxes comes from Social Security benefits. You did NOT read that wrong. $35 BILLION of distributed Social Security Income goes right back to the government in tax money. You paid taxes to save it, but son of gun, unless you make the right moves before you retire, you may end up giving some of the same income you are entitled to from your taxed Social Security income right back. What a deal! Like I said, taxation of Social Security is here to stay and trust me, it's going to get worse. In fact, some estimate that over the next 10 years more than $596 billion in taxes will come from taxed Social Security benefits. But why?

As the story goes, both parties in the early 80s were concerned about the dwindling trust fund ratio which, by 1982, had reached about the 15% level. They calculate the ratio by taking the value of the trust fund at the beginning of the year and dividing it by the expenditures for that year. Not good. Therefore, in 1983, the congress passed HR 1900, the Social Security Amendment Act. Dan Rostenkowski was the Chairman of the house Ways and Means Committee and the sole sponsor of the act. Tip O'Neill was the Speaker of the House, as Vice President under President Reagan, George H W Bush was the Senate President, and Howard Baker was Senate Majority Leader. By the way, Joe Biden was one of 89 Senators who supported taxation of Social Security in 1983. When they expanded the tax again under President Clinton in 1994, once again, Biden voted yes. There, now you know who the villains are! Both sides of the aisle!

Now that's a lot of bad news about Social Security taxation, right? Well, that's true, BUT, there is a loophole. There are thresholds you must meet with taxable income before your Social Security is taxable. The key to creating a Zero income tax plan (or to paying as low an amount of taxes as possible) is to make sure that your taxable (IRA. 401(k), etc.) income is below those thresholds. The interesting thing is that they extended the tax thresholds in 1994 under President Clinton, but they have never been indexed for inflation!

When you are receiving Social Security, there is a calculation of your provisional income. Without getting bogged down with all the minutia surrounding certain types of foreign income and other unusual sources of income that count, it basically says that if your income from interest, IRAs, 401(k)s, an even interest from tax-free municipal bonds (yup, not so tax free after all) exceeds $34,000, you could pay tax on up to 85% of your Social Security income filing as an individual. If you are filing a joint income tax with your spouse and your combined income exceeds $44,000, you could end up paying taxes on up to 85% of your joint Social Security income. If your income as an individual is more than $25,000 but less than $34,000, up to 50% of your Social Security could be taxable, and if you're married filing jointly, as long as your taxable income stays below $44,000, you'll only pay taxes on up to 50% of your Social Security income.

When I was new in the financial industry and I just started learning about taxes, I often heard, as many of you did, I'm sure, that once you retire, you're in a lower tax bracket. That's a very common myth that many people still believe. As if the government eases up on you after you're retired! I even got into a silly over-heated debate about this with a friend's wife, who fancied herself as a financial expert because she worked at a bank. She was absolutely convinced that I was wrong, and that there was a special tax code for retirees! There isn't.

The trick to getting your taxes to zero is to pay attention to all sources of income once you retire. All the things that you think might be just a little problematic, such as bank interest, savings bond interest when you cash them in, pension income, and tax-free municipal bond income, can cause your Social Security income to become taxable. Also, sadly, there are a handful of states that include some level of Social Security income in calculating your state income tax liability. You can get a current list online at SSI.gov.

One of the more insidious reasons you could pay taxes on your social security income is by having realized gains attributable to you in a non-qualified investment account, like a mutual fund. Ever get taxed on a mutual fund where you paid the tax, but never got to spend the money? This could be just the thing that trips the tax wire in a given year, and you never even saw it coming!

When planning for your long-term retirement income, it is wise to do everything you can, to look far ahead in the future to your retirement years to determine what financial moves you might be interested in making now. This includes making small tax decisions now, to save tax headaches later. For example. Let's assume that you have some money you would like to save specifically for retirement that is outside of your company 401(k) plan. There are limits on how much you can place into an IRA if you have a 401(k); and based upon your income, whether you can take that as a deduction. I will try to avoid specific rules for the current law because laws are constantly changing, being revised, and so forth.

If you're reading this at some point when the laws have changed since I published this book, check the current rules with your accountant or financial advisor. The point is this boils down to a very simple decision; pay me now, or pay me later.

Fram Oil Filters had a very successful advertising campaign many years ago when they were plying the logic that paying a little money now for a new oil filter would be much better than paying later for a new engine. Their slogan was, "you can pay me now, or you can pay me later." The same is true for taxes on your retirement funds. If you can put retirement funds into a ROTH IRA where you get no tax deduction today but have unlimited tax-free growth on that money forever, it makes sense to make that decision from a long-term perspective.

Remember my conspiracy theory in the last chapter? It applies here as well! If you invest $7,500 into an IRA at age forty, for example, and you earn 5% interest until you're age 67, your IRA account will be worth about $29,000, all of which is taxable. In exchange for this, you get to adjust your taxable income now, (reduce it) by that $7,500 amount. If you are currently in a 22% effective bracket, married filing jointly, with a combined income of $140,000, you might save as much as $1,800 in taxes now. The trade off, of course, is that you will have to pay taxes on the entire account value in retirement, assuming you withdraw it. Let's assume you have combined Social Security income of $50,000 in retirement, but you need to withdraw that $29,000 to supplement Social Security. You will likely trigger a portion of your Social Security to become taxable.

If, on the other hand, you invest the same money in a Roth, earn the same amount of interest, and take the same amount of money out of your Roth, there is no income tax due on the Roth, and it does not trigger taxation of your Social Security. The good news is that in the example above, in 2023, if you are married filing jointly and your total retirement income is $79,000, ($50,000 Social Security + IRA withdrawal) because you've drawn less than the standard deduction, you pay no taxes on the IRA withdrawal.

But what if you are widowed at retirement? Now you only receive one Social Security check (you lose the lower of the two). In that same scenario, because you lose one of the two Social Security checks, you will likely need to take more from your IRA to make up the difference. You also lose one of your standard deductions. Now, only drawing one Social Security check of, let's say, $30,000 and if you need to get to the same income withdrawing from IRA funds, you will pay over $6,100 in income taxes!

We know we don't live forever and that's why it's so important to deploy long-term strategies for retirement early on. The adage, "if I only knew then what I know now" certainly applies here!

Life Insurance to the Rescue

Now let's step back, and without going into details about types of policies here, (we do that in Chapter 8), let's assume that you are looking for other ways that you can save for retirement which will not impact your taxable income. We recognize Roth IRAs are tax free; so, what else is tax free?

This leads us to the sometimes-highly political debate about why the rich don't pay taxes. There are many things that the wealthy do to avoid income taxes. Instead of worrying about deductions, most of them are very savvy about leverage. Isn't that a cool word? I love it, leverage. Sounds sophisticated, right? Well, all leverage means is that they live on borrowed money! That's right! If you've ever taken a home equity loan, you know you did not owe income taxes on that money. The reason you don't owe taxes is that you borrowed from an asset that has equity (value) that was accumulated with after-tax dollars. You don't have to report it as income. That's a very important financial secret that most of us just don't think about. Therefore, we do what we are told. We work hard. We pay our taxes. We save money in our 401(k) plans, and when we retire, we keep paying. And most of us don't like the thought of getting our income from some other equity source such as a reverse mortgage (although for some people this is a lifesaver), or another home equity loan.

What if we looked at alternative ways to save for retirement other than saving in tax-deferred instruments like IRA accounts, 401(k) accounts, or annuities?

(A word about annuities. As you will see in the next chapter, I am a huge fan of annuities for many reasons, but they can present a tax issue in retirement. And your overall retirement strategy will require that you balance the benefits of annuities, and there are many, versus the potential tax issues they could create. More to come.)

So, what is another way to save for retirement that is tax advantaged besides ROTH accounts? If you read the sub-headline of this section, you guessed it: life insurance. Life insurance cash values can become a fantastic source of tax-free retirement income and in today's financial environment, they can also help to plug other risk holes, since many new cash value life insurance plans offer living benefits as well. I will touch on these later. First, we need to understand a basic financial concept. LIFO vs FIFO.

Oh boy, here we go with the jargon. Well, this one's easy. LIFO stands for Last In, First Out. FIFO stands for First In, First Out. Here's why that's important. Just about everything that creates wealth, whether it be property ownership, savings accounts, annuities, IRAs and retirement plans, stocks, most bonds, second homes, business ownership, you name it; we treat as a LIFO distribution when you liquidate them. If you sell your business for more than you paid for it (assuming with after-tax dollars), then when you sell it, you owe taxes on the gain. You can only avoid that tax on the money you receive on the sale of your business is if you sell it for LESS or equal to what you put into it. What you put into it is called your basis. Anything above that is taxable as a gain. Same goes for rental properties, a non-qualified stock sale, and so forth. In other words, almost every major transaction will have tax consequences on any gains. But not life insurance. If done correctly, of course.

Unless you violate some rules for how you fund the policy, we know it in the industry as a Modified Endowment Contract or MEC, this life insurance product is FIFO. You can withdraw your basis first and then borrow against the remaining cash values. When done right, you pay no tax on this income whatsoever.

You caught me. You cunningly noticed I used the word borrow. So, you're asking, "You want me to borrow my income in retirement?" I shake my head yes, and you say, "What about preaching that I should stay debt free?"

Well, there's an interesting difference in the way and the source of your borrowing and how this borrowing is different.

First, you're not actually borrowing from your policy. You're borrowing from the insurance company and pledging the cash values and death benefit associated with your policy as collateral up to the amount of the loan. Remember earlier I mentioned that with insurance products such as life insurance and annuities, (except for Variable Annuities, which are securities, which, by the way, for various reasons I dislike) you are working under contract law. An insurance policy is as I stated previously, a unilateral contract between the policy owner, usually but not always the person who is the insured, and the insurance company.

Second, you have the contractual right to access cash from the insurance company by pledging your policy as collateral. You must have the cash values in the policy to pledge, but nonetheless, you have property rights with life insurance, by contract! That's why purchasing life insurance is a privilege, not a right. You sign an application, not an order form. The company has the right to decline your application for health, financial, or even moral reasons if they choose. Once you have the contract in hand, however, unless you fraudulently applied, you have a contractually guaranteed financial instrument. The contract guarantees the terms and conditions, not necessarily the performance. Whole life policies, however, do have a guaranteed cash value associated with them. There are small exceptions, usually having to do with small burial policies.

Products have evolved in the life insurance industry for the good in so many ways. There are always things to be aware of, however.

Here is my first major caution regarding your decision to include this miraculous product in your planning. Very few people, and sadly, even some life insurance agents, have a thorough understanding of how to use life insurance properly as a retirement vehicle. The fact is, for the type of life insurance I am going to propose here, Indexed Universal Life (IUL), it is very easy for the policy design to favor the agent's compensation rather than the performance for the consumer. The agent designing your policy must understand and be willing to create a design that greatly favors you, the consumer. This is due in large part to the way the face amount (death benefit payable) is determined. Some policies have limitations on how the plan can be structured, but most IUL policies have a great deal of flexibility in this regard. Make sure that you understand this before you buy an Indexed Universal Life policy. I don't believe that ethical insurance agents are going to pull the wool over your eyes. In my experience most agents are ethical and are quite proud of creating a policy that will benefit you greatly. But, like anything else, buyer beware.

Buying an Indexed Universal Life Policy

I am going to use general rules of thumb here, but these are the most important things to learn BEFORE you meet with an agent to discuss the purchase of a life insurance retirement policy or LIRP. LIRP is not business jargon, it's now a commonly used term in our industry. In fact, I recommend that you read "The Power of Zero, How to Get to a Zero Percent Tax Bracket and Transform Your Retirement" by my friend David McKnight. David gave us the term LIRP!

First, savvy agents design these policies to offer the lowest possible death benefit to allow for the highest possible cash value accumulation. That's good. You want your life insurance retirement policy to be built with a low death benefit so that you can maximize the cash value. This brings me to another serious warning.

We find companies and life insurance salespeople out there who criticize any agent who is selling indexed universal life. They claim these agents sell IULs for the commissions. The critics advocate buying term insurance and investing or saving the difference. (Term insurance has an important role in your planning, but it has no value to anyone unless you die while still within the term) To rely solely on term insurance, in my opinion, is a deeply flawed strategy.

Permit a short soap boxing pause here. "It is also interesting to note that this same type of agent will lead off the discussion with criticism of your agent who sold you the IUL or the whole life policy we discussed earlier by attacking their ethics. Don't you hate that? I distrust someone who sinks to bad-mouth your previous agent, whom they have likely never even met, mind you, to convince you to buy something else? Makes me want to take a shower. Uugh. Oh, and they are most likely a "Regional Vice President" because once they sell you, they try to recruit you. Multi-level marketing nonsense at its zenith." End of soap box.

Your retirement planning is serious business. Work with a professional. I've been in this industry for a very long time. I don't know any wealthy people, successful business owners or CPAs who work with these soap-box types of agents. Professionals comport themselves professionally. There are enough highly ethical and professional agents in this industry who are dedicated to doing what is in your best interest. In future chapters, we will discuss how to find and hire these highly ethical and professional agents.

Also, beware of taking advice from someone outside the industry, even a CPA about life insurance. Most knowledgeable CPAs understand the excellent tax benefits of life insurance, but I've met too many who have highly uninformed opinions about it. A professional agent will be happy to meet with your CPA to provide detailed information about what they are proposing. If your CPA says no, the most logical question then is, "well, how would YOU advise me to get to zero and accomplish the things that this book has taught me?" They will be hard-pressed to give you an alternative strategy; for one reason, it doesn't exist! I've worked with many CPAs who love life insurance and understand it. If you get opinions from someone about this, be sure that they have a better idea and can quantify it.

The reason I am compelled to mention this is that life insurance has become a commodity. You see or hear advertisements from companies who brag about how much they can "save" you on your life insurance purchase. They quote rates for 10-year term insurance, meaning that the policy ends if you don't die within ten years. You will likely need life insurance much longer than 10 years. What they don't mention, and what is important to note is that after 10 years, the policy expires. If you're still alive and if you still need life insurance, you're going to have to pay a lot more and as you age, it gets more and more expensive. I love term insurance for young families. I've owned term insurance, and I use term insurance in my "get me to zero" planning, but permanent life insurance has substantial tax benefits that simply are not found in any other product. When I say that we want the lowest death benefit with our IUL, it's because we want the highest cash accumulation. The lower the death benefit, just at or slightly below the MEC limit, the better for creating tax-free income later in life. Many of my clients have life insurance cash values in the hundreds of thousands of dollars. Not one of them thinks they made a poor decision. Especially in today's economic environment.

Second, be sure that the agent you work with is independent. The sad double-edged sword in the life insurance industry is that most companies have disbanded their sales forces for several reasons, but most commonly due to cost. A good independent agent will probably work with several excellent companies. I have a couple of companies that I prefer for whole life policies and two or three different companies for IUL. Usually, captive agents, those representing only one company, are limited to selling only that company's policies. While not always true, most of the time, those companies do not compete well to satisfy this type of need, especially on the whole life product side of things.

Third, make sure that you are buying from highly rated companies to accomplish these strategies. This is more important than ever before. In fact, I am more and more inclined in my planning to stick with mutual life insurance companies who are owned by their policy owners rather than working with stock companies. This is 100% true for any whole life insurance policies but even for IUL, which is a little trickier for mutual companies to offer. I like mutual companies first. Mutual life insurance companies tend to be a bit more conservative. However, you should not assume that they are in great financial shape just because they are a mutual company. Do your homework. As we plan, we partner with a firm that has created the best insurance company analysis process that I have ever seen.

Fourth, be sure that you meet regularly (and there should never be a fee involved for follow-up meetings and reviews of life insurance if the person doing the review is the person who sold you the policy) to make sure that your initial cash value projections are on track.

Fifth, even though you may not completely understand it, request a copy of the final policy illustration when they deliver your policy. Many companies do that automatically. If the illustration that comes from the company differs from the one the agent went over with you, don't panic. Many times, the agent is using a perfectly good and legal strategy with the policy, but the insurance company doesn't know that, and when they issue your illustration, they send a basic plan illustration.

Finally, DO NOT buy IUL with "minimum premiums". This is NOT a minimum strategy. I like to analyze the difference between having my client continue doing what they're doing (i.e., funding a 401(k), paying their debts as they currently are, not changing a thing) versus what I am proposing as an alternative. Getting to Zero income tax requires a lifetime commitment to a strategy that will free you from government audits, changing tax codes, tax liabilities for beneficiaries and more. (It should look like you have minimal income - LEGALLY of course) This is NOT a minimum strategy. It is different, and it works for many people.

If you think about it, you may pour money every paycheck blindly into a retirement account that nobody advises you on, that you don't understand, and that will create tax issues in the future. With this strategy, you will work with an advisor and together you can plan and adjust through the years.

We've discussed ROTH accounts, and we've discussed IULs as a source of tax-free retirement income. What else will get you to ZERO? There's always a HECM. What's a HECM? It's a Home Equity Conversion Mortgage.

I don't sell HECMs, but I have an opinion. In the right circumstance, I like them. These are otherwise known as reverse mortgages. Dr. Wade Pfau, a professor at the American College, is a huge proponent of reverse mortgages. I will not get into the weeds in this book about them other than to say that these are the criteria I like to consider when I might want to recommend that my client consider a reverse mortgage.

All a reverse mortgage really is, is a way for you to access the equity in your home on a tax-free basis. They are useful tools for many reasons and there are arguments for and against them. You can take the money out of your home in a reverse mortgage in typically one of three ways:

1. You take a lump sum. I rarely recommend this. However, there is a school of thought that says taking as much equity out as you can and saving it somewhere else is a way to protect your equity in a declining housing market. I don't like using this strategy. I don't recommend it.

2. You can take a tax-free monthly income check. I think this is a worthwhile consideration as a last resort.

3. You can create a line of credit with the approved reverse mortgage and have it there for emergencies. I like this one a lot.

You should talk to a certified reverse mortgage specialist, and I believe it wise to have your other advisors in on the conversation. I listed the plus sides above. The downsides are:

1. The initial interest and costs are significant. While you can just have that money taken from the reverse mortgage account, they will charge it interest and that loan against your property will grow every year at a stipulated interest rate.

2. The reverse mortgage company will have to be paid in full once you leave your home. That's why you should seldom do a reverse mortgage if you're not planning for you and your spouse to stay in that home for the rest of your lives. Carefully check the terms and conditions for paying off the reverse mortgage if you decide to sell or downsize.

3. You must maintain the home up to FHA standards since the FHA guarantees the bank issuing the reverse mortgage that it will make them whole at the end of the deal. You could get a reverse mortgage, for example, based upon your home being worth, let's say, $500,000. But what if housing prices collapse or decline? You're usually fine as long as you stay to the end because the Federal mortgage insurance issued as part of your deal will make up any deficiency. In other words, the bank could never demand more from your survivors than the value of the home.

Reverse mortgages do make sense for some people and if you are considering one, I highly recommend that you look up Wade Pfau on the internet and read what he says about reverse mortgages. He's the authority on this in my view.

So, there you have it, three places for income, ROTHs, Life Insurance and reverse mortgages where you can say to uncle Sam regarding the income, you can't touch this!

Chapter Six

Chutes and Ladders....

About 200 years before the birth of Jesus Christ, there was in India a game known as Snakes and Ladders. Here is how it is described in Wikipedia;

> *"The game was popular in ancient India by the name Moksha Patam. It was also associated with traditional Hindu philosophy contrasting Karma and Kama, or destiny and desire. It emphasized destiny, as opposed to games such as pachisi, which focused on life as a mixture of skill (free will) [7] and luck."*

This game is the basis for the popular American game known as *Chutes and Ladders.*

I find this to be quite an appropriate metaphor for retirement income planning. I know, makes me a little weird but hang in there.

As you can see from the definition, on the one hand, we have Karma. Almost everyone I know has some vague understanding that Karma is basically the balancing of one force against another. Often in spirituality it is used to describe the offsetting of one's lessons from one lifetime to another, the Ying and the Yang of life so to speak. Those who believe in Karma, believe that you balance your good and bad deeds often from one lifetime to the next. In other words, Karma is your destiny.

However, if you remove the "r", now you have Kama which is all about desire. Yes, it does have to do with all kinds of desire, but relax, this is a family friendly book! I believe there is no better way to understand what's going on in our heads when we start thinking about retiring. What do we want when we retire?

The third zero, in the get me to zero strategy, is all about reducing or even eliminating risk associated with investing. Does that mean I advocate that you don't invest in the markets? The real answer has to do with how the other two Zeros are working. Once you have zero debt, and you've basically planned for Zero income taxes, or at least the lowest possible, you are now in a place where the accumulation and more importantly the decumulation of money in safe buckets become the next objectives in the Get Me to Zero strategy.

I am often asked by clients, prospective clients, golf buddies on the course (and I really hate talking about business on the golf course, since I am always trying to lower my golf handicap and want to focus on golf!), or wherever I might be once they learn about what I do for a living, what I think is going to happen in the market. I'm sure I don't need to say this, but here goes anyway, nobody knows what's going to happen in the market! I don't care who claims to have predicted what as so many gurus try to make you believe. It is unknowable. I submit however that if you think about it, your money will show you both your Kama, as well as your Karma after a long enough period of time.

Do we not have desires that only money can help us to attain? You want that boat, or vacation home, or next flashy car. You want that feeling of never having to worry about money ever again. These are deep desires. This is Kama.

On the other hand, you might be making some money decisions that created some Karmic debt. Or maybe you wasted money frivolously for many years on things that only satisfied your Kama. Now, as you get closer to retirement, maybe you find yourself a bit unprepared and perhaps woefully behind in your savings. That is Karma.

By the way, if you ever hear me speak live and I'm discussing the difference between Karma, and Kama, you won't know which one I'm referring to because I'm from New England. We like dropping our "r's". Don't be afraid to make me clarify!

The Social Security Decision

Once we start getting close to our retirement age, we start to take inventory of what we have as possible sources of income. Most of us have Social Security. For baby boomers, Social Security income represents about 40% of their monthly income in retirement. Here's the conclusion of an excellent study by the Social Security Administration entitled: "The Changing Impact of Social Security on Retirement Income in the United States", by Barbara A. Butrica, Howard M. Iams, and Karen E. Smith.

"Conclusion"

"The Social Security Administration's MINT (Monthly Income Near Term) model projects measures of well-being through 2032 for birth cohorts born between 1926 and 1965. Using projections of income at age 67 from MINT, this analysis assesses the role of major government income programs in the economic well-being of baby-boomer retirees and their predecessors. The analysis focuses on Social Security and SSI benefits and their contribution to overall income since Social Security, in particular, is likely to be affected by social, demographic, and labor market changes that have transformed retirement expectations for the baby boom cohort. The analysis suggests that baby boomers can expect higher incomes and lower poverty rates at retirement than current retirees have. Similar to current retirees, Social Security will account for about two-fifths of projected total income and will be received by almost all baby-boomer retirees. SSI, which on average contributes almost nothing to total income, will be received by 5 percent of current retirees and only 2 percent of baby boomer retirees."

Did you catch the compounding variables? Social Security will be affected by social, demographic, labor market changes.

The projections also suggest that baby boomers born between 1946 and 1964 will likely receive the most generous benefits in history. If you're a boomer, congratulations! For the rest of you, retirement income planning has never been more important. How you think about retirement is highly influenced by media, advisors, friends and yes, brother-in-laws! Your Social Security decision encompasses many considerations such as what your provisional income will be once you take it and how that will impact the amount, if any, of your Social Security will be subject to taxation. (By the way, most states do not tax Social Security Benefits. There are a handful of states that do.) What follows is all part of making that decision, but first it is wise to make sure we understand some important issues as we plan for retirement income.

Chutes

Even though the majority opinion in America surrounding growing your money and your wealth has largely revolved around investing in stocks and bonds; for the purposes of my argument here, I propose that we need to revisit the magic of compound interest as a "financial society" if you will allow me to coin that term.

There's a reason why Albert Einstein referred to compound interest as the 8th wonder of the world! Forgive me for being so basic here, but after 43 years of working with folks in the retirement income space and seeing what market investing bias has done to the way people understand money, I believe this is needed. Even if you already understand compound interest, let's consider the following.

One of my favorite sites online for a neutral third-party calculator for money concepts is a site called MoneyChimp.com. On their site, you can perform all kinds of calculations. One of my favorite ones is the Compound Annual Growth Rate (CAGR) calculator. You can find it here. http://moneychimp.com/features/market_cagr.htm

(Many of the examples that follow are using the returns found in the above calculator.)

What has happened over the years, since the creation of the 401(k) which invited so many Americans to blindly invest in cool sounding mutual funds, is that Wall Street has gotten away with promoting average rates of returns on investments. The problem is average rates of return are NOT convertible into actual monetary results. Here's the example that MoneyChimp.com uses to explain average rates of return. I used to do this exact calculation all the time for my clients, and then I saw it on this site! I will just quote their site since I would explain this the same exact way.

"If you had an investment that went up 100% one year and then came down 50% the next, you certainly wouldn't say that you had an average return of 25% = (100% - 50%)/2, because your principal is back where it started: your real annualized gain is zero.

In this example, the 25% is the simple average, or "arithmetic mean." The zero percent that you really got is the "geometric mean," also called the "annualized return," or the CAGR for Compound Annual Growth Rate.

Volatile investments are frequently stated in terms of the simple average, rather than the CAGR that you actually get. (Bad news: the CAGR is smaller.)"

Now, if I told you that you were going to get an average rate of return of 25%, you would likely jump at such an opportunity. Why wouldn't you? But as you can see, average rates of return are highly susceptible to skewing the results. Once you understand how the geometric mean works, it is important to understand what you can expect with various investments, at least from a volatility standpoint.

When you are discussing this with your advisor, I think it is critical to understand the geometric mean, or better stated, the compound annual growth rate (CAGR). There is a calculation to determine risk. It's known as the standard deviation. While there are many ways to evaluate investments and investment portfolios, and even though I understand that standard deviation is only one measurement of the performance of an equity-based portfolio, but in my opinion, it is the most reliable and the one most likely to impact retirement income. The reason? Chutes and ladders!

In retirement income planning, we use the term "glide path" to estimate the decumulation of assets as income. How smooth will the glide path be? The glide path will be bumpy if you're only trying to remove the same percentage of income by selling stocks and bonds because every time you do, you will be selling a different number of shares. If the share prices drop while you're drawing income, you must sell more shares to achieve the same income. If you are drawing down in a declining market, and you are drawing down a fixed dollar amount, you are negative dollar cost averaging. More and more shares need to be sold as the prices of the equities in your portfolio decline. Your glide path when drawing the income then is smooth, but there could be a cliff at the end because you no longer have any shares left. This is a chute off the cliff!

If you are drawing down a fixed percentage of a declining portfolio, then your glide path will not be so sweet. For example, let's assume you want to draw down 5% of $100,000. For purposes of this illustration, we will assume 0% interest to understand the concept.

Month 1, you withdraw $5,000 from your $100,000 portfolio, and that leaves a balance of $95,000. In month 2, you draw down 5%

of the balance, and now you receive $4,750 ($95,000 X 5%). Month 3, you take another 5% of the remaining balance of $90,250 and you receive $4,512.50 ($90,250 X 5%) and so on. As you can see, in an inflationary time, this is unsustainable. Before you know it, you're broke! This is a descending ladder!

Now, let's add another variable, (remember compounding variables?) and assume that you received the actual returns of the Standard and Poor's 500 index WITH dividends from the years 2000, 2001, and 2002 AFTER each withdrawal. (refer to Moneychimp.com CAGR Example).

Year	Balance	5% Withdrawal	Balance	Market Results	New Balance
2000	$100,000.00	$5,000.00	$95,000.00	-9.11%	$86,345.50
2001	$86,345.50	$4,317.28	$82,028.23	-11.98%	$72,201.24
2002	$72,201.24	$3,610.06	$68,591.18	-22.27%	$53,315.92

Chart 6.1

So after just three years of negative dollar cost averaging, your account balance is down by $46,684.08. ($100,000 - $53,315.92) Of that amount, you withdrew a total of $12,927.94 (sum of 5% withdrawals for three years). This is a bumpy glide path at best and the chute is not looking so hot. Your account took a total hit of $46,684.08! You only got to spend $12,927.94. How long do you want to keep doing this? Better yet, how long can you keep doing this?

What if you had an account that paid just 3% interest on that money. What would it look like? Even if you earned the interest AFTER taking the withdrawal.

Year	Balance	5% Withdrawal	Balance	Interest Paid	New Balance
2000	$100,000.00	$5,000.00	$95,000.00	$2,850.00	$97,850.00
2001	$97,850.00	$4,892.50	$92,957.50	$2,788.73	$95,746.23
2002	$95,746.92	$4,787.34	$90,959.57	$2,728.79	$93,688.36

Chart 6.2

In the first scenario, your account is down $46,684.08 and you got to spend $12,927.94. In this scenario above, your account took a total hit of $6,311.64 ($100,000 - $93,688.36) and you got to spend $14,679.84 (Sum of 5% withdrawals). This is a difference of $40,372.44! (End of Year 3 in Chart 6.2 – end of year 3 in chart 6.1) How many

$40,372.44 hits to your accounts are you willing to endure hoping the markets come raging back to save you?

Even if you're not a math wizard, it's easy to see that you are in much better shape in the second scenario. And while I'll touch on this more in the next two chapters, consider what if you also had to pay a combined federal and state tax of 15% on the income because the above are IRA accounts which are fully taxable when you withdraw the funds? You want to withhold the taxes from the income. What happens now if you "gross up the withdrawal" to get the net 5% in your pocket after taxes?

Here's the sneaky little IRS trick. You would think that you need to gross up your withdrawal by the 15% of the amount you want. Not so! 15% of $5,000 is $750. If I add $750 to $5,000, I get $5,750. $5,750 X's 15% = $862.50. $5,750 - $862.50 =$,4,887.50. Uh oh, I'm short $112.50 for the $5,000 I need! Now I must gross up more to net my $5,000. The calculation for that number is $5,000 / 85% (100 – 15% tax bracket). Therefore, I must withdraw $5,882.35. 85% of $5,882.35 = $5,000. Now let's look at the results.

Year	Balance	5% Withdrawal	Gross Withdrawal Income	15% Tax On Withdrawal	Balance	Market Results	New Balance
2000	$100,000.00	$5,000.00	$5,882.35	$882.35	$94,117.65	-9.11%	$85,543.53
2001	$85,543.53	$4,277.18	$5,031.98	$754.80	$80,511.35	-11.98%	$70,866.09
2002	$70,866.09	$3,543.30	$4,168.59	$625.30	$66,697.50	-22.27%	$51,843.97

Chart 6.3

Can you see how this becomes an ever-spiraling situation for a retiree, especially in a down market? Now the damage to the account is even greater! You spent $12,820.48 (sum of 5% withdrawals). You withdrew $15,082.92 (sum of gross withdrawals) to net it after taxes, and then the market went down a total of 43.36%. (sum of market results) You lost $33,072.91 to the market. This my friends, is a worst-case type of scenario. But every year, your portfolio performed within two standard deviations! (I explain standard deviation below, remember this!) For this reason, it is a realistic scenario as well! In this example you're down almost half of your money, but you only got to enjoy $12,820.48! Is my conspiracy theory starting to make sense? In addition, multiply this example by making the numbers 5 or 6 times higher in all categories if you have an account worth $500,000 or $600,000 instead of the example of $100,000! If you take out taxable income that is more than your standard deductions, your

Social Security now becomes partially taxable.

With the interest of 3%, here's how it looks when we add the taxes.

Year	Balance	5% Withdrawal	Gross Withdrawal Income	Tax On Withdrawal	Balance	Interest Paid	New Balance
2000	$100,000.00	$5,000.00	$5,882.35	$882.35	$94,117.65	$2,823.53	$96,941.18
2001	$96,941.18	$4,847.06	$5,702.42	$855.36	$91,238.76	$2,737.16	$93,975.92
2002	$93,975.92	$4,698.80	$5,530.00	$829.19	$88,445.92	$2,653.38	$91,099.30

Chart 6.4

Here, your portfolio is down due to withdrawals and taxes plus 3% on remaining balances each year by $8,900.70. ($100,000 - $91,099.30) You withdrew a total of $17,114.77 (Sum of Gross withdrawals) pretax. You got to spend $14,545.86 (Gross withdrawals less taxes) after taxes. Your account value is still only down $8,900.70 after a total withdrawal of $17,114.77. The 8th wonder of the world at work! By the way, if you let this portfolio sit for just under 3 years at 3%, it would grow back to your original $100,000.

This is why I believe that as you enter retirement you want zero risk on your income producing investments to stabilize your retirement with the feeling that you're still getting a paycheck, but you're no longer working for it. That paycheck, which will help with the Kama, or your desires for a wonderful retirement, whether you spend it on what you enjoy, save it for a special vacation or trip, (do you still call a trip a vacation once you're retired? Hmmm), as the source of income to pay specific bills, or whatever you deem to be a good use of money.

You will note that in BOTH scenarios above, whether we used a market-based account or even with a low interest-based account, the year over year income was dwindling, because we wanted a fixed interest rate withdrawal of 5% of the balance. We were trying to live on a 5% withdrawal factor because we heard somewhere that you could take 4% of your portfolio as income safely and the money would last until life expectancy. Maybe you thought, as many of us do, that you were not going to live that long, and you could take 5% instead! The result was reverse inflationary income. In other words, we were falling behind year over year. While clearly, we need to consider the safety of our money, we also need to be realistic and we must find better ways to create our income streams in retirement so that they don't dwindle, but in fact they increase.

As you can see, compound interest is a huge help in the above scenarios, but we still are in trouble if we're trying to keep up with inflation. That is why I believe that in the last 5 to as long as 10 years before you retire, it's time to really begin plans to keep what you have. The entire Get Me to Zero strategy is focused first on your being able to recapture money you use to pay down debt. Once that's done and the focus moves to tax reduction strategies, we want to get your income tax liability down as close as we can to Zero, and that means no more having to "gross up" our withdrawals as you see above for tax purposes. Therefore, a tax-free pile of money starts to look extremely inviting!

When you're making these critically important retirement decisions, it's not enough to rely upon average rates of return. I once was at an advisor's conference for training on my retirement planning software. I always found that conference to be the best I attended since to understand the use of the software, it is necessary to understand how money and various products work in general. At this event, the presenter was showing a case study and using average rates of return for the retirement assets. The software provides the ability to insert a risk range or standard deviation calculator for those same assets. When I prepare a retirement income plan, it usually involves an analysis of the existing portfolio to obtain important data such as finding out what the standard deviation of the portfolio is. We also want to know what the product charges if any (mutual fund or ETF fees for example) are, as well as any other fees. You see, in the above example, if the money is in the market, and you're paying even a 1% fee to the fund or the advisor. It gets even uglier.

In the next example, I gave the investments the benefit of the doubt because I did not include fees for the investments. But what if you are in fact paying a 1% management fee? Here's how the IRA draw-down looks if we add in an advisor fee of just 1%. (This is going to vary from advisor to advisor. Both the amount of the fees, and the time as to when they get charged could be different.) For purposes of our discussion, and to give lower fees the benefit of the doubt, let's only charge the fee after the grossed-up withdrawal for taxes. I'll even only charge the fee AFTER the market losses (which would not likely happen).

Year	Balance	5% Withdrawal	Gross Withdrawal Income	Tax On Withdrawal	Balance	Market Results	New Balance	Fee of 1%	Net Balance
2000	$100,000	$5,000	$5,882	$882	$94,117	-9.11%	$85,543	$855	$84,688
2001	$84,688	$4,277	$5,032	$755	$80,511	-11.98%	$70,866	$709	$70,157
2002	$70,157	$3,543	$4,168	$625	$66,697	-22.27%	$51,843	$518	$51,325

Chart 6.5

So now we've accounted for poor market returns, taxes, and advisor fees. But many investments also have fees! It's possible that you could have as much as another 1% to 1.5% in mutual fund or exchange traded fund fees! I think you get the point. By the way, with the advent of the exchange traded fund option to the average investor, I wonder why anyone would pay the higher fees to own a similar mutual fund! That's just a question, not investment advice.

Now these scenarios above are not so great, but they are also not the way clients withdraw money in my experience. I have never in my career had a client tell me to just send them 5% of their account value each year for example. I have had them tell me they wanted $5,000 a year, every year, and adjusted for inflation too! Oh boy, now we're really looking at compounding variables! Let's take our last scenario, with the fees, (I will still not include an assumed fee for the fund so there still would be that to consider. In all my planning however, we do include the impact of all fees on any accounts we use), but now let's take a level $5,000 from our IRA, not just 5% of the account value, and let's assume we want 3% more each year for inflation. Here's what that looks like;

Year	Balance	5% Withdrawal 3% Inflation	Gross Withdrawal Income	Tax On Withdrawal	Balance	Market Results	New Balance	Fee of 1%	Net Balance
2000	$100,000	$5,000	$5,882	$882	$94,117	-9.11%	$85,543	$855	$84,688
2001	$84,688	$5,150	$6,059	$909	$78,629	-11.98%	$69,209	$692	$68,517
2002	$68,517	$5,305	$6,241	$936	$62,276	-22.27%	$48,407	$484	$47,923

Chart 6.6

In this scenario, as you can see, it gets worse still. You are taking more income each year, but that increases the gross withdrawal amount which increases the taxes. Those two variables alone create another serious drag on your income. This market-based solution doesn't look great and yes, I am using three historically bad years in the example. But there's a reason for that. Hope is not a strategy. I learned a very long time ago, that hope can only be a strategy if we plan for the worse first. Plan for the worse, hope for the best. I'm sure you know I didn't make that one up! That, I can live with. By contrast, here's what this looks like with a 3% interest bearing account.

Year	Balance	5% Withdrawal 3% Inflation	Gross Withdrawal Income	Tax On Withdrawal	Balance	Interest Paid	New Balance
2000	$100,000	$5,000	$5,882	$882	$94,117	$2,823	$96,940
2001	$96,940	$5,150	$6,059	$909	$90,881	$2,726	$93,607
2002	$93,607	$5,305	$6,241	$936	$87,366	$2,621	$89,987

Chart 6.7

In this example, an interest rate as low as 3% instead of hoping for a great market return, makes a difference of $42,064! That's not chump change. Therefore, when advising clients as to when to take Social Security, it is my job to figure all of this out first! There are many questions to answer about this money before we can make the social security decision.

How confident are we that there will be an income stream from an asset and for how long? Will that asset, in this case an IRA, possibly cause taxation of Social Security? Can we safely withdraw from this asset for a specified period without having to draw on Social Security?

The decision then for deciding on when to take Social Security starts in my view with answers to those questions and then modeling that in our planning software with different Social Security filing scenarios. If we're confident that waiting will be a benefit but the income that would be provided by a Social Security check in retirement still needs to be there from some other source, then how much of our savings are we willing to use in order to wait another year or two or longer to start taking our Social Security income?

If we wait to take Social Security and we have IRA, 401(k) money along with an after-tax mutual fund or investment portfolio and perhaps some savings, which pile of money should we use first? Does it make sense to delay our Social Security longer and live first on our retirement savings, all of which are taxable as income but won't create a tax on our Social Security? Social Security benefits will grow by 8% for every year we wait until the required minimum distribution age. Where else can you guarantee an 8% increase in income year over year plus cost-of-living adjustments! Of course, the 8% increase stops once you begin receiving your benefit, but it sure makes waiting attractive! Now you can see, the decision on when to take Social Security is important and is impacted by you guessed it, compounding variables!

Ladders

What about the savings side of the coin? Well, once again, I refer you to my friends at MoneyChimp.com. We see there that we can find out what the returns were over the past however many years we want to choose. I can almost hear the argument from investment folks over my examples above. "He's using one of the worst crashes in history by using returns from 2000, 2001, and 2002. Of course, it would look bad!" If your plan is to hope we get consistent positive market returns, you have a hope-based strategy. And friends, hope ain't a strategy.

Let's consider this from the accumulation standpoint. If the S&P 500 index has a compound annual growth rate of 4.26% since the year 2000, and it has a standard deviation of 17.55, without dividends (see MoneyChimp.com CAGR of the S&P 500 since 2000 to 2022) and 6.25% and 18.06 standard deviation) with dividends, the question becomes, "Am I willing to take this amount of risk, in order to expect this kind of return?"

You see, this means that 66% of the time, with dividends, your investment returns in any given time period can fluctuate between, losing 11.81% (-11.81 – +24.31) to making as much as 24.31%. Two deviations for the next 30% or so of the time, you could fluctuate between losing 29.87% (-29.87% - 42.37%) or making as much as 42.37%! Finally, about 4% of the time, think 2008, you can be outside 2 standard deviations. In a roaring market, your investments could consistently perform at the higher end of one deviation quite consistently like in the 1990's. Approaching the second deviation on the upside, especially for a number of consecutive years is wonderful for existing portfolios, but not great for those folks who are dollar cost averaging into the market. As prices climb, the number of shares you can buy gets smaller, and yet, a rising market makes everyone feel good. In a falling market, you could be at the far end of that same deviation such as 2002. Even the most novice of investors understands that you should buy low and sell high. The question is, who knows what kind of market it will be and for how long? Therefore, when climbing the savings ladder for retirement, the question arises, is it better to invest and hope, or should I save in an interest-bearing account?

Let's take a quick look at a compound interest chart to understand the point. It is my contention that as a financial society, we have forgotten the amazing power of compound interest.

Deposits and Withdrawals			Withdrawal Rate			Deposits and Withdrawals		Interest Rate	
								3.00%	Yr 1
D	$500,000	Portfolio	0.00%	Tax Rate	D	$500,000	3.00%		Base
W	$0	Growth	Account	15.00%	W	$0		Growth Rate	Account
Year	Tax Free	Rate	Value		Year	Taxable			Value
0	$500,000	S&P 500	$500,000		0	$500,000			$500,000
1	$0	-10.14%	$449,300		1	$0	3.00%		$515,000
2	$0	-13.04%	$390,711		2	$0	3.00%		$530,450
3	$0	-23.33	$299,558		3	$0	3.00%		$546,364
4	$0	26.38%	$378,582		4	$0	3.00%		$562,754
5	$0	8.99%	$412,616		5	$0	3.00%		$579,637
6	$0	3.00%	$424,995		6	$0	3.00%		$597,026
7	$0	13.60%	$482,794		7	$0	3.00%		$614,937
8	$0	3.52%	$499,788		8	$0	3.00%		$633,385
9	$0	-38.49%	$307,420		9	$0	3.00%		$652,387
10	$0	23.65%	$380,125		10	$0	3.00%		$671,958
11	$0	12.63%	$428,134		11	$0	3.00%		$692,117
12	$0	0.10%	$428,563		12	$0	3.00%		$712,880
13	$0	13.29%	$485,519		13	$0	3.00%		$734,267
14	$0	29.43%	$628,407		14	$0	3.00%		$756,295
15	$0	11.64%	$701,553		15	$0	3.00%		$778,984
16	$0	0.73%	$706,675		16	$0	3.00%		$802,353
17	$0	9.54%	$774,091		17	$0	3.00%		$826,424
18	$0	19.42%	$924,420		18	$0	3.00%		$851,217
19	$0	-6.24%	$866,736		19	$0	3.00%		$876,753
20	$0	28.88%	$1,117,049		20	$0	3.00%		$903,056
		5.68%					3.00%		

Chart 6.8

I call this little tool "The Double Dilemma" because when I use the excel version to have this conversation with a client, I can change the variables and include taxes, or not include taxes. In this example, we are not saving yearly. We have a sum of $500,000 to invest or save. If we decided to invest on January 1, of the year 2000 in the S&P 500 index, our average rate of return as seen at the bottom of the third column is 5.68%. That is derived from adding all the returns each year and dividing by 20. In this example, we would end up with $1,117,049. In other words, over 20 years, our money would have more than doubled! That's awesome!

In the column on the right, the money earns 3% compound interest and after 20 years has grown to $903,056. If I asked the obvious question, "which do you prefer?" I'm pretty sure there would be more people who favor the market-based column on the left since the result is more than $200,000 better. That is very understandable. Now, let's look at what happens if we need to take 5% of the portfolio or $25,000 per year, as income. In other words, on January 1 of 2000, you started taking income.

	Deposits and Withdrawals	Withdrawal Rate			Deposits and Withdrawals	Interest Rate 3.00%	Yr 1
D	500,000	Portfolio	5.00%	Tax Rate	D	$500,000	3.00%	Base
W	$25,000	Growth	Account	15.00%	W	$25,000	Growth	Account
Year	Tax Free	Rate	Value		Year	Tax Free	Rate	Value
0	$500,000	S&P 500	$500,000		0	$500,000		$500,000
1	$25,000	-10.14%	$424,300		1	$25,000	3.00%	$489,250
2	$25,000	-13.04%	$343,971		2	$25,000	3.00%	$478,178
3	$25,000	23.33%	$238,723		3	$25,000	3.00%	$466,773
4	$25,000	26.38%	$276,698		4	$25,000	3.00%	$455,026
5	$25,000	8.99%	$276,573		5	$25,000	3.00%	$442,927
6	$25,000	3.00%	$259,870		6	$25,000	3.00%	$430,465
7	$25,000	13.60%	$270,213		7	$25,000	3.00%	$417,629
8	$25,000	3.52%	$254,724		8	$25,000	3.00%	$404,407
9	$25,000	-38.49%	$131,681		9	$25,000	3.00%	$390,790
10	$25,000	23.65%	$137,823		10	$25,000	3.00%	$376,763
11	$25,000	12.63%	$130,230		11	$25,000	3.00%	$362,316
12	$25,000	0.10%	$105,361		12	$25,000	3.00%	$347,436
13	$25,000	13.29%	$94,363		13	$25,000	3.00%	$332,109
14	$25,000	29.43%	$97,134		14	$25,000	3.00%	$316,322
15	$25,000	11.64%	$83,440		15	$25,000	3.00%	$300,062
16	$25,000	0.73%	$59,049		16	$25,000	3.00%	$283,314
17	$25,000	9.54%	$39,683		17	$25,000	3.00%	$266,063
18	$25,000	19.42%	$22,389		18	$25,000	3.00%	$248,295
19	$22,389	-6.24%	$0		19	$25,000	3.00%	$229,994
20	$0	28.88%	$0		20	$25,000	3.00%	$211,143

Chart 6.9

As you can see here, when taking income, even though the average rate of return was higher on the market side, you run out of money after 18 years, and even in year 18, you can't take your full withdrawal. On the right side, with just a 3% return, you can withdraw $25,000 every year for 20 years, which by the way is $500,000, and you still have over $200,000 remaining!

If I gross up the withdrawals for taxes as in our earlier examples, you can imagine the gap gets wider.

Deposits and Withdrawals		Withdrawal Rate			Deposits and Withdrawals	Interest Rate 3.00%	Yr 1
D 500,000	Portfolio	5.00%	Tax Rate	D $500,000	3.00%	Base
W $25,000	Growth	Account	15.00%	W $25,000	Growth	Account
Year Tax Free	Rate	Value		Year Taxable	Rate	Value
0 $500,000	S&P 500	$500,000		0 $500,000		$500,000
1 $29,412	-10.14%	$419,888		1 $29,412	3.00%	$484,706
2 $29,412	-13.04%	$335,723		2 $29,412	3.00%	$468,953
3 $29,412	-23.33%	$227,987		3 $29,412	3.00%	$452,727
4 $29,412	26.38%	$258,718		4 $29,412	3.00%	$436,015
5 $29,412	8.99%	$252,565		5 $29,412	3.00%	$418,801
6 $29,412	3.00%	$230,731		6 $29,412	3.00%	$401,071
7 $29,412	13.60%	$232,698		7 $29,412	3.00%	$382,809
8 $29,412	3.52%	$211,477		8 $29,412	3.00%	$364,000
9 $29,412	-38.49%	$100,668		9 $29,412	3.00%	$344,625
10 $29,412	23.65%	$95,064		10 $29,412	3.00%	$324,670
11 $29,412	12.63%	$77,659		11 $29,412	3.00%	$304,116
12 $29,412	0.10%	$48,325		12 $29,412	3.00%	$282,945
13 $29,412	13.29%	$25,335		13 $29,412	3.00%	$261,140
14 $25,335	29.43%	$7,456		14 $29,412	3.00%	$238,680
15 $7,456	11.64%	$0		15 $29,412	3.00%	$215,546
16 $0	0.73%	$0		16 $29,412	3.00%	$191,718
17 $0	9.54%	$0		17 $29,412	3.00%	$167,176
18 $0	19.42%	$0		18 $29,412	3.00%	$141,897
19 $0	-6.24%	$0		19 $29,412	3.00%	$115,860
20 $0	28.88%	$0		20 $29,412	3.00%	$89,041

Chart 6.10

Here you can see that with the market returns on the left, you are out of money in just 15 years, and in year 14, you can only withdraw about 25% of what you need. With 3% interest on the other hand, you still have $89,041 and you have taken out $588,240 ($29,412 X 20 years) including the gross up for taxes.

Here is another way to look at compound interest.

A very wise mentor of mine by the name of Nelson Nash who created the Infinite Banking system that many people find works well to manage and grow their wealth, said something very revealing to me regarding compound interest. He told me that the rate didn't matter, but the volume did. What? The rate didn't matter, but the volume did? If we look at chart 6.11 you can see what he meant.

	Invested	Age	Interest Rate	Interest On Original	Growth Interest	New Balance	Cumulative Interest	Cumulative Interest On Original
	$500,000.00		3.50%					
Year	Year	Age	VOLUME					
1	2020	60	$17,500.00	3.50%	$17,500.00	$517,500.00	$17,500.00	3.50%
2	2021	61	$18,112.50	3.62%	$612.50	$535,612.50	$35,612.50	7.12%
3	2022	62	$18,746.44	3.75%	$633.94	$554,358.94	$54,358.94	10.87%
4	2023	63	$19,402.56	3.88%	$656.13	$573,761.50	$73,761.50	14.75%
5	2024	64	$20,081.65	4.02%	$679.09	$593,843.15	$93,843.15	18.77%
6	2025	65	$20,784.51	4.16%	$702.86	$614,627.66	$114,627.66	22.93%
7	2026	66	$21,511.97	4.30%	$727.46	$636,139.63	$136,139.63	27.23%
8	2027	67	$22,264.89	4.45%	$752.92	$658,404.52	$158,404.52	31.68%
9	2028	68	$23,044.16	4.61%	$779.27	$681,448.68	$181,448.68	36.29%
10	2029	69	$23,850.70	4.77%	$806.55	$705,299.38	$205,299.38	41.06%
11	2030	70	$24,685.48	4.94%	$834.77	$729,984.86	$229,984.86	46.00%
12	2031	71	$25,549.47	5.11%	$863.99	$755,534.33	$255,534.33	51.11%
13	2032	72	$26,443.70	5.29%	$894.23	$781.978.03	$281,978.03	56.40%
14	2033	73	$27,369.23	5.47%	$925.53	$809,347.26	$309,347.26	61.87%
15	2034	74	$28,327.15	5.67%	$957.92	$837,674.42	$337,674.42	67.53%
16	2035	75	$29,318.60	5.86%	$991.45	$866,993.02	$366,993.02	73.40%
17	2036	76	$30,344.76	6.07%	$1,026.15	$897,337.78	$397,337.78	79.47%
18	2037	77	$31,406.82	6.28%	$1,062.07	$928,744.60	$428,744.60	85.75%
19	2038	78	$32,506.06	6.50%	$1,099.24	$961,250.66	$461,250.66	92.25%
20	2039	79	$33,643.77	6.75%	$1,137.71	$994,894.43	$494,894.43	98.98%

Chart 6.11

Let's first notice that we're starting once again with an initial sum of $500,000. In the fourth column from the left, you see the word volume. Notice that even though the interest rate stays the same at 3.5%, the volume of interest keeps growing in that column. In the column next to it, you see what that year's interest is and what rate it would be on the original $500,000 investment. For example, look at year 10. The 3.5% rate on that year's balance produces $28,850.70 of interest. That's the equivalent of 4.77% that year on the original money! The column on the far right calculates the cumulative interest or growth on the original amount. For example, in year 10, the interest has accumulated to $205,299.38 which is 41.06% higher than the beginning value. Think hard about what I just said. If your investment advisor told you that he could guarantee growth of 41.06% on your investment in just 10 years, would you think that was a reasonably good goal for a return? Well, here it is. No investment fees, and more importantly ZERO risk. This is the true power of Zero risk.

The argument I am making here is that in my opinion, whenever we can help our clients to achieve reasonable returns with Zero risk, we are obligated to at least discuss it and compare it to the alternative. I also believe that your advisor should do the same. I believe that risk tolerance is a major discussion point in any financial advisory relationship. I also believe that it is completely appropriate, and the law now requires that your advisor be willing to disclose their compensation and how it varies according to which products you use in your plan.

Retirement is full of KAMA, at least that's what many of our clients relate to us. We love hearing about the cruises, the time with the grandchildren, the enjoyment of their lives. This is desire. This is good. This is supported by a smooth glide path or chute if you will.

The ladder is more about how you save for retirement. It's about numerous major financial decisions you will make throughout your lifetime on the road to retirement. You will create KARMA on the way, and believe me when I tell you, in retirement it's all about reaping what you've sown on the way.

Talk to your advisor about compound interest options on your ACTUAL money, not just on some other account that is only used for income like an income rider on an annuity!

Beware of this one common misunderstanding about some types of annuities. I will often have a potential client show me a variable annuity statement (I'm not a big fan of variable annuities) and the account value is down from the initial premium and they tell me they don't understand because the advisor told them it would earn 6% or 7% or whatever rate guaranteed! What they aren't so clear about is that the compound interest is on a rider that can ONLY be taken as income. The actual money is invested in what I consider to be almost without exception, sub-par sub accounts or mutual fund accounts. Clients almost always think they are earning the guaranteed interest on the actual premium they invested. This is the kind of thing that gives annuities a bad reputation. Understanding what you are buying is an important thing!

I love using other types of annuities for retirement planning. I just don't love variable annuities for many reasons. It is interesting to note that many large insurance companies have sold off their variable annuity book of business. The reason is that the risk to the insurance company is far higher than the fees charged to allow them to safely reserve for their liabilities. This doesn't make the broker bad or insurance company bad per se, but it does however speak to the added risk of these products that I just feel is unnecessary and dangerous when planning for retirement.

I do like fixed indexed annuities. Many fixed indexed annuities offer attractive riders and I love those also, and the premium is never subject to market loss. In higher interest rate environments, I LOVE multi-year guaranteed annuities or MYGAs. As I write this in 2023, MYGA rates are very attractive. Here's another advisor secret. We get paid less, many times far less, depending upon the length of time you have surrender charges. THIS SHOULD NEVER BE A CONSIDERATION FROM YOUR ADVISOR! I know that by doing the right thing, good things happen for everyone involved.

The bottom line here is that you will have the Chutes and Ladders acting in your financial life until the end. The game was derived from the snakes and ladders KAMA versus KARMA version in India some 2,500 years ago. Desire vs Destiny. How appropriate.

Chapter Seven

Off to See the Wizard... or A Financial Advisor?

I remember it like yesterday. I was about 6 or 7 years old and my grandmother, who sadly was widowed from my paternal grandfather for many years, bought the first color television in our entire family. Wow, what a treat it was to go to her house to watch "The Wizard of Oz," and seeing the colors of Munchkin Land for the first time! It was like nothing I had ever seen. It was magical.

I've always loved the story of the Wonderful Wizard of Oz. There are so many metaphors in the story, but as just about everyone who has ever seen the movie can attest, the irony is that each character in the story already possessed the talent or gift they were seeking from the wizard. The scarecrow is obviously the smartest of Dorothy's new friends. The tin man is obviously a softhearted guy, and even the cowardly lion musters up the courage to help save Dorothy. Dorothy learns she has hidden power in her ruby slippers to get home, and the wizard, who wasn't a wizard after all, fulfills the wishes of all involved with a little common sense. It's a timeless story that I hope lives a long time in the repertoire of magical children's stories. There are many lessons for children in that story, and many for us adults too!

When you think about planning your financial life, I can't imagine what it must be like for the folks who only care about what money does, and not so much about how it all works. The greatest metaphor in the Wizard of Oz is, of course, the instruction to "follow the yellow brick road." At the end, you will find a great wizard who will give you what you desire. But where's the yellow brick road for retirement planning? How do you even know what questions to ask? And who do you trust along the way?

Do you procrastinate planning because you either don't know how or aren't sure what you're even worried about? It's dizzying. Add to that the fact that there is so much noise shouting what is "best" for your financial life. "Buy stocks and bonds." "Invest in BitCoin." "Time to buy gold and silver." "Invest in renewable energy stocks." "Buy real estate." And as I write these words in 2023, it's the same week as the failure of two major banks, Silicon Valley & Signature. The list goes on and on, and so do the folks behind the stories.

The real question is, what is your true KAMA, or desire financially? Money is one of those things, like politics, where everyone has an opinion and most of them stink. This book, and this financial philosophy of getting to zero debt, zero income taxes, and zero risk, is about helping you to find your yellow brick road to what I love to call FREEtirement, the great Emerald City. When you owe nothing, have no income-tax liability, and can do well withdrawing income without investment risk, your mind and your life become free of financial worry.

I'm sure that at this point you would like a full "how to get it done" instruction manual. The thing is, there are many ways to get to zero. I believe all those fortunate to experience the wonderful feeling of FREEtirement, whether their road was yellow brick, dirt or hot pavement, had to navigate the many compounding variables! And by the way, many of those clients got there without me!

It was a common thing for early baby boomers to have parents that never had a credit card, paid cash for their cars, and likely never moved from the first house they purchased. If they were super lucky, they had an annuity, which is another word for a company pension. Most pension plans give you a choice of "annuity income," or a "lump sum." In my experience I find that annuities are greatly misunderstood, and it is the one financial product that gets criticized the most and usually for the wrong reasons. Many times, the criticism comes from someone with a competing goal, like an investment advisor who says, "I hate annuities, and so SHOULD you!" There's that should word again. I urge you to keep an open mind about annuities, I don't love them all, but they have great utility in a retirement income plan. When folks worked for a company with a pension, they would work longer hours, stay a few more years, and work as hard as possible, perhaps with lots of overtime just to maximize their pensions! What they were really doing was trying to get the highest ANNUITY payment possible.

These folks knew that the key to financial security is to do the basic things to get that special peace of mind that comes with knowing that "they can't hurt me". Let them raise taxes! I have no taxable income! Let the market crash! I have no risk! I can listen to the nightmare of how much debt the country is in, but if my "personal economy" is free of all debt, I guess that's not my problem either. We all know people who live like this. Many live beautiful and simple lives and they are free from the need for financial worry. That's where I would like you to be someday. But as I think about this, I'm reminded of another concept in that wonderful book, "*The Psychology of Money*" which is "the seduction of pessimism." It is this most dangerous truth that I must warn you about here as well.

Without rewriting or at the risk of copying what Housel says in his book about this subject, allow me to share one of the most important things I hope you learn from reading this book. Listen, study, and read on your own about your financial situation. I can't even count the number of hours I have spent with clients and prospective clients discussing some crazy opinion that a friend, uncle, parent or whoever had about certain financial decisions, products, and investments. Just because someone believes something fervently and with apparent authority, doesn't mean that they are an authority on a financial decision you are grappling with! If someone has had a terrible experience, it is THEIR experience. But you know what? As humans, we love group misery. If your opinionated friend shares an experience they had with something you're thinking about, continue to consider it yourself. They want you to rubber neck their disaster while they tell you all about it. Don't do it. You oversee your own financial destiny. Period.

Here's an example. You decide after doing your research that you are going to dedicate much of your savings' dollars to buy strong whole life policies for you and your spouse. You've done your research and based upon the suggestions and questions to ask an advisor, which I've provided in the back of this book, you've selected the company, the premium you will pay, and are now moving forward on that decision. You tell your uncle, brother-in-law or whomever about it. They react negatively and tell you that "whole life stinks." They go on about the low return rates and how it's much better to buy term insurance (which you purchase with protection dollars, and which I wholeheartedly endorse in many circumstances) and "invest" the difference.

The fundamental problem is that you are now confusing a SAVINGS objective with an INVESTMENT objective. They are NOT the same. But you become convinced that perhaps you are making the wrong move. So often, opinions are NOT based on facts, and sometimes having a little knowledge about something is more dangerous than being an expert. You learn that whole life insurance is an amazing creation by the actuaries of life insurance companies and has been around successfully for over 200 years. When you understand how it works and why, it is a perfect place for accomplishing multiple goals, which I will touch on later. At this point, don't be swayed by some half-baked opinion from someone who is ignorant of all the facts.

We can say the same about investments. For example, you may be convinced that owning an Exchange Traded Fund (ETF), which perhaps focuses on growth stocks, is an easy way to gain exposure to the market in an important investment sector. Then someone tells you that you're better off with individual stocks instead. The correct answer for you is whether you feel competent to manage an individual stock portfolio, or are just as happy to have an Exchange Traded Fund (ETF) to handle the investment sector for you. There are good reasons one may work better for you than the other. Ultimately, this must be your call and your call only. I am a huge fan of ETFs instead of mutual funds, but some people feel better with the structure of mutual funds. You're not crazy as Housel says, but you do oversee your own financial destiny, and ultimately you are responsible for the outcome. It's your yellow brick road, keep learning.

People love to share negative experiences they've had and in the spirit of trying to help you avoid "the same mistake," they raise doubts in your mind. The problem is you may not know the complete story behind their experience. I hear this all the time about annuities, for example.

There are many types of annuities. We know one of the more commonly sold annuities as variable annuities. I am not a huge fan of variable annuities for several reasons. For one reason, these products tend to have significantly higher fees than other investments. But most of the time, I believe the fees do not justify the risk. But even I need to be sure that I am hearing the complete story before I make a blanket recommendation. For example, I recently met with a wholesaler from a company I highly respect, and have had splendid success with on the fixed annuity side. Although I have never liked variable annuities, he told me about a variable annuity product they have that made me understand I may paint with too broad a brush. As an advisor, I must always be open to looking at something different, even if I have an opinion already. While you need to do the same and not close your mind to an alternative you may not have considered, it doesn't mean that the alternative is going to be better than what you've already decided to do.

But how do you know? That's where your evaluation of your advisor comes in. You need an advisor with whom you travel the yellow brick road together. Otherwise, like Dorothy and her companions, you see the glistening Emerald City and charge off through a field of distractions. Believe me, there are plenty of fields of distraction.

To stay true to the yellow brick journey—which I remind you is to get to zero and enjoy FREEtirement, you are the one responsible. It is important you understand how some of the subtle misunderstandings of interest, savings, inflation, taxes, drawdowns, deviations, risk, averages, and their other flying companions can carry you off the road and into financial captivity.

For the rest of this chapter, let's explore how some of these distractions, or better said, misunderstandings, can easily lure you into the field of confusion.

Assuming you decide you want to be "FREEtired" as soon as possible, and together with your advisor, you commit to achieve that goal. Then, with any financial option you consider, like a variable annuity, or a mutual fund, or individual savings tools, you must ask, "How will this help Get Me to Zero?"

Remember, I argue in this book that one of the three zeros is the zero risk for assets that you need to live off in your retirement years. I don't mean that you might not have investments in your portfolio, but I do mean zero risk when you are drawing them down, or as we like to say, taking income from them. If someone advises you to make a financial move in contrast to that aim, it is up to you to evaluate it in the context of your overall goal of getting to zero. You can ask your advisor very specific questions how violating the zero-risk principle would be beneficial to you. Before retirement, of course, it is prudent to make investments that involve some risk. Usually, the risk reward equation comes into play, and you must make a determination whether it fits for your situation. Investing in your 401(k), usually means selecting some risk-based investments with the understanding that your money could grow faster, yet you could lose value if the market declines. The point is, and this is not always the easiest thing to understand, you are buying shares in your 401(k) by investing your money. You are NOT SAVING money when you invest, and you are NOT earning compound interest when you invest. You hope you are buying stocks and bonds that reach and maintain their highest values after you retire, so that when you need income from them, the higher value of your investments will mean that you sell fewer shares to get the same dollars you spent while you were investing. Beware of any financial advisor, publication, or brochure that confuses the terms investing and saving. I've seen them used interchangeably and they are NOT the same thing.

I repeat! The important thing is that when you have made your Get Me to Zero decision, you need to work with an advisor who will help you stay on track to reach those goals, not try to change your mind. Having and following a plan is critical. Follow the yellow brick road, so to speak.

In my planning, I have software that allows me to do the most important thing almost everyone needs to do when deciding; compare one set of assumptions against the other. This is how I like to handle the discussion of compounding variables. And trust this, in retirement planning there are nothing but compounding variables!

Let me illustrate and examine one simple goal in retirement. Assume for a moment that our client has exactly $500,000 saved for retirement. He needs to draw $25,000 or 5% of the original amount from this account to last as long as possible in his retirement and he's wondering what to do. For simplicity, we assume the funds are in his IRA account. The money is currently in a cash account and now it's time to deploy it, which means; put it to work.

The Misunderstanding of Average Rates of Return.

The first question is, if he invests it, what returns might make sense to help him with his decision? I mentioned earlier that one of the most significant mistakes that many advisors make, is their plan designs have an average rate of return for assets invested in the market. This could be a serious mistake if the sequence of returns doesn't work in your favor. This dangerous assumption could create an illusion that you are going to be able to retire safely because there is an assumed constant "average" rate of return. If the returns are substantially lower, especially when you first start taking income, it can mean that the plan is off by several years!

A note about sequence of returns: Though an average rate of return may be positive over a twenty-year period, the sequence of returns, whether positive or negative, greatly impact the actual final dollars in your pocket. In some of the following examples, we'll show you how dramatically they affect your retirement cash.

Chart 7.1 below shows what the S&P 500 index returns look like, assuming our client retired on January 1, 2000, and invested his retirement in the Standard & Poor's 500 index. After all, the 90's were tremendous for growth in the market! These are the returns without dividends. I will show examples with dividends later. The software allows us to provide data from which it will illustrate our projected retirement withdrawals. Each field lets us make assumptions or provide historical data.

Year	Age	Defined Contribution Plan
1	67	-10.36%
2	68	-13.23%
3	69	-23.52%
4	70	27.47%
5	71	9.57%
6	72	3.54%
7	73	14.49%
8	74	4.21%
9	75	-38.47%
10	76	25.86%
11	77	13.62%
12	78	0.82%
13	79	14.63%
14	80	31.18%
15	81	11.83%
16	82	-0.55%
17	83	8.29%
18	84	20.69%

Average yield: 3.90%

CHART 7.1

We choose to rely on the S&P 500 previously stored yield schedules. We could also determine level or random yields if we chose. Relying on the S&P 500 previously stored yield schedules since 2000, we see the average yield is 3.90%. (While this is different than the average you see in the Money Chimp software, it is the average when repeating the same return pattern until age 100, when in this case, the full cycle has not repeated. These averages can also be changed by the software based upon the numbers of years and how much of the sequence is repeated.)

Using these yields which average 3.90%, if our client needed to withdraw $25,000 per year from this account every year—using this sequence of returns; here is what it would look like.

Retirement Assets Initial Value 500,000		Retirement Plan Assets Cost Basis 0		Retirement Plan Account Yield See Col. 4		Retirement. Income Tax Rate 0.00%	
Year	M/F Ages	(1) Beginning of Year Plan Assets	(2) Before Tax Required Minimum Distribution	(3) Before Tax Distribution	(4) Retirement Plan Assets Yield (Avg. 4.87%)	(5) After Tax Cash Flow from Retirement	(6) Year End Retirement Plan Assets
1	67/67	500,000	0	25,000	-10.36%	25,000	425,790
2	68/68	425,790	0	25,000	-13.23%	25,000	347,765
3	69/69	347,765	0	25,000	-23.52%	25,000	246,851
4	70/70	246,851	0	25,000	27.47%	25,000	282,793
5	71/71	282,793	0	25,000	9.57%	25,000	282,464
6	72/72	282,464	0	25,000	3.54%	25,000	266,578
7	73/73	266,578	10,060	25,000	14.49%	25,000	276,583
8	74/74	276,583	10,846	25,000	4.21%	25,000	262,175
9	75/75	262,175	10,658	25,000	-38.47%	25,000	145,934
10	76/76	145,934	6,158	25,000	25.86%	25,000	152,208
11	77/77	152,208	6,647	25,000	13.62%	25,000	144,534
12	78/78	144,534	6,570	25,000	0.82%	25,000	120,514
13	79/79	120,514	5,712	25,000	14.63%	25,000	109,488
14	80/80	109,488	5,420	25,000	31.18%	25,000	110,831
15	81/81	110,831	5,713	25,000	11.83%	25,000	95,985
16	82/82	95,985	5,188	25,000	-0.55%	25,000	70,595
17	83/83	70,595	3,988	25,000	8.29%	25,000	49,375
18	84/84	49,375	2,939	25,000	20.69%	25,000	29,418
19	85/85	29,418	1,839	25,000	-7.49%	25,000	4,087
20	86/86	4,087	269	4,087	0.00%	4,087	0
21	87/87	0	0	0	0.00%	0	0
22	88/88	0	0	0	0.00%	0	0

Chart 7.2

Note that the client is out of money in 20 years, and the last year for the full withdrawal is year 19. If our client goes to his or her

Retirement Plan Assets Initial Value 500,000		Retirement Plan Assets Cost Basis ➡		Retirement Plan Assets Yield 3.90%	Retirement Income Tax Rate 0.00%	
Year	M/F Ages	(1) Beginning of Year Plan Assets	(2) Before Tax Required Minimum Distribution	(3) Before Tax Distribution	(4) After Tax Cash Flow from Retirement Plan Assets	(5) Year End Retirement Plan Assets
1	67/67	500,000	0	25,000	25,000	493,525
2	68/68	493,525	0	25,000	25,000	486,797
3	69/69	486,797	0	25,000	25,000	479,807
4	70/70	479,807	0	25,000	25,000	472,544
5	71/71	472,544	0	25,000	25,000	464,998
6	72/72	464,998	0	25,000	25,000	457,158
7	73/73	457,158	17,251	25,000	25,000	449,012
8	74/74	449,012	17,608	25,000	25,000	440,548
9	75/75	440,548	17,908	25,000	25,000	431,754
10	76/76	431,754	18,217	25,000	25,000	422,617
11	77/77	422,617	18,455	25,000	25,000	413,124
12	78/78	413,124	18,778	25,000	25,000	403,261
13	79/79	403,261	19,112	25,000	25,000	393,013
14	80/80	393,013	19,456	25,000	25,000	382,366
15	81/81	382,366	19,710	25,000	25,000	371,303
16	82/82	371,303	20,070	25,000	25,000	359,809
17	83/83	359,809	20,328	25,000	25,000	347,867
18	84/84	347,867	20,706	25,000	25,000	335,459
19	85/85	335,459	20,966	25,000	25,000	322,567
20	86/86	322,567	21,222	25,000	25,000	309,172
21	87/87	309,172	21,470	25,000	25,000	295,255
22	88/88	295,255	21,551	25,000	25,000	280,795
23	89/89	280,795	21,767	25,000	25,000	265,771
24	90/90	265,771	21,785	25,000	25,000	250,161
25	91/91	250,161	21,753	25,000	25,000	233,942
26	92/92	233,942	21,661	25,000	25,000	217,091
27	93/93	217,091	21,494	25,000	25,000	199,583
28	94/94	199,583	21,009	25,000	25,000	181,392
29	95/95	181,392	20,381	25,000	25,000	162,491
30	96/96	162,491	19,344	25,000	25,000	142,853
31	97/97	142,853	18,314	25,000	25,000	122,449
32	98/98	122,449	16,774	25,000	25,000	101,250
33	99/99	101,250	14,890	25,000	25,000	79,224
34	100/100	79,224	12,379	25,000	25,000	56,339

Chart 7.3

glorious reward around age 85, not bad!

You see in column 4 the yield varies from the high of 31.18% in year fourteen and a low of -38.47% in year nine, yet the average of 4.87% still beat the projected 3.90%. Regardless, at 85 years old, the account is dry.

Now, chart 7.3 (previous page) displays what this would look like if we used an actual fixed 3.90% rate of return every year, rather than the fluctuating rates which swung wildly year to year. Remember, the actual yield is different from the average. Yield is equivalent to the Compound Annual Growth Rate. (CAGR).

You might think, how could this be? You see how at age 100, there's still money in the account! It is the magic of compound interest, but more importantly, it demonstrates how erroneous assumptions in your retirement plan can have disastrous consequences!

A common retirement planning mistake is assuming that a fixed, consistent 3.90% rate of return is the same as an average 3.90% return in the market where an unpredictable poor sequence of returns could decimate your cash.

But other compounding variables like taxes, inflation, etc., can make it even worse. Remember, this is retirement income from an IRA account which, no matter where it is invested, is going to be taxable.

So, let's look at it with taxes included. What if the effective rate is 22% on this money? Chart 7.4 (pg. 85) shows what the market return example looks like if we add in taxes. And we need to draw more out to cover the taxes and net the same $25,000 per year.

If we added taxes in at this level, notice that the money runs out in 13 years instead of the 19 without taxes. With such a short period, higher returns later do not offset the poor market returns early in the timeline. Thus, an average yield of 1.17% using poor market returns adds to the shrinking plan assets. If we compare that to the consistent fixed 3.90% yield interest rate and we include taxes, it looks like this in chart 7.5 (pg. 86).

In both scenarios, we have the same tax rate, however, with a compound interest rate equal to the average rate of return of the market, our client gets an additional 10 years of income!

		Retirement Plan Assets Initial Value 500,000	Retirement Plan Assets Cost Basis 0		Retirement Plan Account Yield See Col. 4	Retirement Income Tax Rate 22.00%	
		(1)	(2)	(3)	(4)	(5)	(6)
Year	M/F Ages	Beginning of Year Plan Assets	Before Tax Required Minimum Distribution	Before Tax Distribution	Retirement Plan Assets Yield (Avg. 1.17%)	After Tax Cash Flow from Retiremen Plan	Year End Retirement Plan Assets
1	67/67	500,000	0	32,051	-10.36%	25,000	419,469
2	68/68	419,469	0	32,051	-13.23%	25,000	336,163
3	69/69	336,163	0	32,051	-23.52%	25,000	232,585
4	70/70	232,585	0	32,051	27.47%	25,000	255,621
5	71/71	255,621	0	32,051	9.57%	25,000	244,966
6	72/72	244,966	0	32,051	3.54%	25,000	220,452
7	73/73	220,452	8,319	32,051	14.49%	25,000	215,700
8	74/74	215,700	8,459	32,051	4.21%	25,000	191,381
9	75/75	191,381	7,780	32,051	-38.47%	25,000	98,036
10	76/76	98,036	4,137	32,051	25.86%	25,000	83,049
11	77/77	83,049	3,627	32,051	13.62%	25,000	57,944
12	78/78	57,944	2,634	32,051	0.82%	25,000	26,105
13	79/79	26,105	1,237	26,105	0.00%	20,362	0
14	80/80	0	0	0	0.00%	0	0
15	81/81	0	0	0	0.00%	0	0
16	82/82	0	0	0	0.00%	0	0
17	83/83	0	0	0	0.00%	0	0
18	84/84	0	0	0	0.00%	0	0
19	85/85	0	0	0	0.00%	0	0
20	86/86	0	0	0	0.00%	0	0

Chart 7.4

We already know what a zero-tax rate looks like since in the first two examples, there was no tax. It is also important to note that every tax scenario will be unique. It's also important to note that an effective rate of 22% is probably high in 2023 before any changes to the tax law, but consider where you think tax rates might be going!

What if you could only get your taxes lower by 40% instead of getting all the way to zero? Would that help? Let's look at chart 7.6 (pg. 87) to see what market returns with a 13.2% (40% lower) effective tax rate. In the market-based scenario, you see the results.

As you can see, just by reducing the taxes by 40%, the client gets almost three more years of income. With the consistent 3.90% interest rate, it looks like the results in chart 7.7 (pg. 88).

Here, the dual power of compound interest with lower taxes

		Retirement Plan Assets Initial Value 500,000	Retirement Plan Assets Cost Basis 0	Retirement Plan Assets Yield 3.90%	Retirement Income Tax Rate 22.00%	
		(1) Beginning of Year Plan Assets	(2) Before Tax Required Minimum Distribution	(3) Before Tax Distribution	(4) After Tax Cash Flow from Retirement Plan Assets	(5) Year End Retirement Plan Assets
Year	M/F Ages					
1	67/67	500,000	0	32,051	25,000	486,199
2	68/68	486,199	0	32,051	25,000	471,860
3	69/69	471,860	0	32,051	25,000	456,962
4	70/70	456,962	0	32,051	25,000	441,483
5	71/71	441,483	0	32,051	25,000	425,400
6	72/72	425,400	0	32,051	25,000	408,690
7	73/73	408,690	15,422	32,051	25,000	391,328
8	74/74	391,328	15,346	32,051	25,000	373,289
9	75/75	373,289	15,174	32,051	25,000	354,546
10	76/76	354,546	14,960	32,051	25,000	335,072
11	77/77	335,072	14,632	32,051	25,000	314,839
12	78/78	314,839	14,311	32,051	25,000	293,817
13	79/79	293,817	13,925	32,051	25,000	271,975
14	80/80	271,975	13,464	32,051	25,000	249,281
15	81/81	249,281	12,850	32,051	25,000	225,702
16	82/82	225,702	12,200	32,051	25,000	201,203
17	83/83	201,203	11,367	32,051	25,000	175,749
18	84/84	175,749	10,461	32,051	25,000	149,302
19	85/85	149,302	9,331	32,051	25,000	121,824
20	86/86	121,824	8,015	32,051	25,000	93,274
21	87/87	93,274	6,477	32,051	25,000	63,611
22	88/88	63,611	4,643	32,051	25,000	32,791
23	89/89	32,791	2,542	32,051	25,000	769
24	90/90	769	63	769	600	0
25	91/91	0	0	0	0	0

Chart 7.5

is worth another three and half years of income above what they would receive in the market average yield scenario.

There are, of course, more compounding variables. For example, the market returns would likely require that a fee be considered.

		Retirement Plan Assets Initial Value 500,000	Retirement Plan Assets Cost Basis 0	Retirement Plan Account Yield See Col. 4		Retirement Income Tax Rate 13.20%%	
		(1)	(2)	(3)	(4)	(5) After Tax	(6)
Year	M/F Ages	Beginning of Year Plan Assets	Before Tax Required Minimum Distribution	Before Tax Distribution	Retirement Plan Assets Yield (Avg. 4.27%)	Cash Flow from Retirement Plan Assets	Year End Retirement Plan Assets
1	67/67	500,000	0	28,802	-10.36%	25,000	422,382
2	68/68	422,382	0	28,802	-13.23%	25,000	341,509
3	69/69	341,509	0	28,802	-23.52%	25,000	239,158
4	70/70	239,158	0	28,802	27.47%	25,000	268,141
5	71/71	268,141	0	28,802	9.57%	25,000	262,244
6	72/72	262,244	0	28,802	3.54%	25,000	241,706
7	73/73	241,706	9,121	28,802	14.49%	25,000	243,754
8	74/74	243,754	9,559	28,802	4.21%	25,000	224,001
9	75/75	224,001	9,106	28,802	-38.47%	25,000	120,106
10	76/76	120,106	5,068	28,802	25.86%	25,000 25,000	114,915
11	77/77	114,915	5,018	28,802	13.62%	25,000	97,842
12	78/78	97,842	4,447	28,802	0.82%	25,000	69,606
13	79/79	69,606	3,299	28,802	14.63%	25,000	46,774
14	80/80	46,774	2,316	28,802	31.18%	25,000	23,576
15	81/81	23,576	1,215	23,576	0.00%	20,464	0
16	82/82	0	0	0	0.00%	0	0
17	83/83	0	0	0	0.00%	0	0
18	84/84	0	0	0	0.00%	0	0
19	85/85	0	0	0	0.00%	0	0
20	86/86	0	0	0	0.00%	0	0

Chart 7.6

There is no fee for most financial instruments that pay compound interest, so let's just take the ZERO scenario (the first one) and add in a 1.25% fee. This will vary greatly from advisor to advisor. Many of the well-known brokerage firms or investment advisors charge about 1% or 1.25%, but you also need to consider that the investments themselves may have small fees. For simplicity, we'll just use a 1.25% fee. You will note that the fee is "hidden" in the numbers, just like in real life scenarios. Also, we will not include taxes. Here are the results in chart 7.8 (pg. 89).

Here, the 1.25% fee costs the client three and a half years of income compared to our very first example above!

Another compounding variable is inflation. The $25,000 withdrawal is level for all these years in this retirement scenario, but

		Retirement Plan Assets Initial Value 500,000	Retirement Plan Assets Cost Basis 0	Retirement Plan Account Yield See Col. 4	Retirement Income Tax Rate 13.20%%

Year	M/F Ages	(1) Beginning of Year Plan Assets	(2) Before Tax Required Minimum Distribution	(3) Before Tax Distribution	(4) After Tax Cash Flow from Retirement Plan Assets	(5) Year End Retirement Plan Assets
1	67/67	500,000	0	28,802	25,000	489,575
2	68/68	489,575	0	28,802	25,000	478,743
3	69/69	478,743	0	28,802	25,000	467,489
4	70/70	467,489	0	28,802	25,000	455,796
5	71/71	455,796	0	28,802	25,000	443,647
6	72/72	443,647	0	28,802	25,000	431,024
7	73/73	431,024	16,265	28,802	25,000	417,909
8	74/74	417,909	16,389	28,802	25,000	404,282
9	75/75	404,282	16,434	28,802	25,000	390,124
10	76/76	390,124	16,461	28,802	25,000	375,414
11	77/77	375,414	16,394	28,802	25,000	360,130
12	78/78	360,130	16,370	28,802	25,000	344,250
13	79/79	344,250	16,315	28,802	25,000	327,750
14	80/80	327,750	16,225	28,802	25,000	310,607
15	81/81	310,607	16,011	28,802	25,000	292,795
16	82/82	292,795	15,827	28,802	25,000	274,289
17	83/83	274,289	15,497	28,802	25,000	255,061
18	84/84	255,061	15,182	28,802	25,000	235,083
19	85/85	235,083	14,693	28,802	25,000	214,326
20	86/86	214,326	14,100	28,802	25,000	192,759
21	87/87	192,759	13,386	28,802	25,000	170,351
22	88/88	170,351	12,434	28,802	25,000	147,069
23	89/89	147,069	11,401	28,802	25,000	122,879
24	90/90	122,879	10,072			97,746
25	91/91	97,746	8,500	28,802	25,000	71,633
26	92/92	71,633	6,633	28,802	25,000	44,501
27	93/93	44,501	4,406	28,802	25,000	16,311
28	94/94	16,311	1,717	28,802	14,158	0
29	95/95	0	0	0	0	0
30	96/96	0	0	0	0	0
31	97/97	0	0	0	0	0
32	98/98	0	0	0	0	0
33	99/99	0	0	0	0	0
34	100/100	0	0	0	0	0

Chart 7.7

Retirement Plan Assets Initial Value 500,000	Retirement Plan Assets Cost Basis 0		Retirement Plan Account Yield See Col. 4	Retirement Income Tax Rate 0.00%	

Year	M/F Ages	(1) Beginning of Year Plan Assets	(2) Before Tax Required Minimum Distribution	(3) Before Tax Distribution	(4) Retirement Plan Assets Yield (Avg. 4.27%)	(5) After Tax Cash Flow from Retirement Plan Assets	(6) Year End Retirement Plan Assets
1	67/67	500,000	0	25,000	-10.36%	25,000	420,468
2	68/68	420,468	0	25,000	-13.23%	25,000	338,858
3	69/69	338,858	0	25,000	-23.52%	25,000	237,038
4	70/70	237,038	0	25,000	27.47%	25,000	266,906
5	71/71	266,906	0	25,000	9.57%	25,000	261,743
6	72/72	261,743	0	25,000	3.54%	25,000	242,060
7	73/73	242,060	9,134	25,000	14.49%	25,000	245,406
8	74/74	245,406	9,624	25,000	4.21%	25,000	226,814
9	75/75	226,814	9,220	25,000	-38.47%	25,000	122,624
10	76/76	122,624	5,174	25,000	25.86%	25,000	
						25,000	121,334
11	77/77	121,334	5,298	25,000	13.62%	25,000	108,087
12	78/78	108,087	4,913	25,000	0.82%	25,000	82,721
13	79/79	82,721	3,920	25,000	14.63%	25,000	65,339
14	80/80	65,339	3,235	25,000	31.18%	25,000	52,255
15	81/81	52,255	2,694	25,000	11.83%	25,000	30,098
16	82/82	30,098	1,627	25,000	-0.55%	25,000	5,007
17	83/83	5,007	283	5,007	0.00%	5,007	0
18	84/84	0	0	0	0.00%	0	0
19	85/85	0	0	0	0.00%	0	0
20	86/86	0	0	0	0.00%	0	0

Chart 7.8

inflation will act like an additional tax. Even though you probably don't want to see the numbers, chart 7.9 (pg. 90) shows what it looks like when you add in just 2% annual inflation to the market returns, with a 22% tax, and a fee. Can you imagine if inflation hovers around current and/or recent levels?

I told you it was ugly. In fairness, chart 7.10 (pg. 91) displays what the consistent 3.90% fixed rate of return is with inflation and a 22% tax rate, but of course there is no fee.

Here you can see how that really makes a difference, however this still outperforms the historical market-based returns with inflation, and by a substantial sum! Of course, market returns could be much higher. The operative word being "could." Your retirement plan "could" be much better than what we are showing

| | | | | | | | Retirement Plan Assets Initial Value 500,000 | | Retirement Plan Assets Cost Basis 0 | | Retirement Plan Account Yield See Col. 4 | | Retirement Income Tax Rate 22.00% |

Year	M/F Ages	(1) Beginning of Year Plan Assets	(2) Before Tax Required Minimum Distribution	(3) Before Tax Distribution	(4) Retirement Plan Assets Yield (Avg. -0.04%)	(5) After Tax Cash Flow from Retirement Plan Assets	(6) Year End Retirement Plan Assets
1	67/67	500,000	0	32,051	-10.36%	25,000	414,226
2	68/68	414,226	0	32,692	-13.23%	25,000	326,919
3	69/69	326,919	0	33,346	-23.52%	26,010	221,718
4	70/70	221,718	0	34,013	27.47%	26,530	236,277
5	71/71	236,277	0	34,694	9.57%	27,061	218,114
6	72/72	218,114	0	35,387	3.54%	27,602	186,831
7	73/73	186,831	7,050	36,095	14.49%	28,154	170,420
8	74/74	170,420	6,683	36,817	4.21%	28,717	137,487
9	75/75	137,487	5,589	37,553	-38.47%	29,291	60,721
10	76/76	60,721	2,562	38,304	25.86%	29,877	27,861
11	77/77	27,861	1,217	27,861	0.00%	21,732	0
12	78/78	0	0	0	0.00%	0	0
13	79/79	0	0	0	0.00%	0	0
14	80/80	0	0	0	0.00%	0	0

Chart 7.9

here. Once again, however, I want to help my clients to plan for the worst while hoping for the best. If the plan works with the bad scenarios, imagine how much better it will be if I am wrong about the taxes being this high, inflation not compounding, and returns being much better than shown!

Of course, the reader could argue that I am using the worst possible starting point for the markets. No doubt by starting the market scenarios with a rising market instead, things would look much better! In fact, I will provide random returns for the market here using a 6.25% compound annual growth rate within the standard deviation, which would look like chart 7.11 (pg. 92). In fact, in my example, I will only look at 1 deviation to minimize the downside.

For those of you who chose a creative major in college, such as art, music, drama, politics, you athletes, or if you skipped out of the math and statistics classes, let me define a standard deviation. Simply, a standard deviation is a way to look at how far numbers

		(1)	(2)	(3)	(4)	(5)
Retirement Plan Assets Initial Value 500,000	Retirement Plan Assets Cost Basis 0		Retirement Plan Assets Yield 3.90%		Retirement Income Tax Rate 22.00%	
Year	M/F Ages	Beginning of Year Plan Assets	Before Tax Required Minimum Distribution	Before Tax Distribution	After Tax Cash Flow from Retirement Plan Assets	Year End Retirement Plan Assets
1	67/67	500,000	0	32,051	25,000	486,199
2	68/68	486,199	0	32,692	25,500	471,194
3	69/69	471,194	0	33,346	26,010	454,924
4	70/70	454,924	0	34,013	26,530	437,327
5	71/71	437,327	0	34,694	27,061	418,336
6	72/72	418,336	0	35,387	27,602	397,884
7	73/73	397,884	15,014	36,095	28,154	375,899
8	74/74	375,899	14,741	36,817	28,717	352,306
9	75/75	352,306	14,321	37,553	29,291	327,028
10	76/76	327,028	13,799	38,304	29,877	299,984
11	77/77	299,984	13,100	39,071	30,475	271,089
12	78/78	271,089	12,322	39,851	31,084	240,256
13	79/79	240,256	11,387	40,649	31,706	207,392
14	80/80	207,392	10,267	41,462	32,340	172,401
15	81/81	172,401	8,887	42,291	32,987	135,184
16	82/82	135,184	7,307	43,137	33,647	95,637
17	83/83	95,637	5,403	44,000	34,320	53,651
18	84/84	53,651	3,194	44,879	35,006	9,114
19	85/85	9,114	570	9,114	7,109	0
20	86/86	0	0	0	0	0

Chart 7.10

may vary from the average they help produce.

So, in using one deviation, I knock off the extremes at both ends which typically includes 66% of the closest numbers to the average. Two deviations reach out and include 96% of the numbers, including those on the extreme edges. Three deviations are out of the most common range of two standard deviations for an investment portfolio. By sticking with one deviation, we can remain more predictable.

In other words, let's say I own a bakery and each morning I

rise early and bake 100 loaves of bread. Each night I count how many loaves I sell and how many sit on the shelf. On Monday, I sell 77 loaves. On Tuesday, I sell 88 loaves, on Wednesday, I sell 64 loaves, on Thursday 92, on Friday 71, on Saturday 91. And so, it goes throughout the month. When I total the sales for the month and divide it by 31, my average sales are 80 loaves of bread. For you math majors, that's 80% average.

Now, the standard deviations are how far from 80 loaves average, the highest and lowest numbers vary from the average or mean, as we call it. One standard deviation goes out and gathers up 34% of the numbers in both directions, or 68% of the daily sales. One standard deviation lets our baker count on more consistent sales. The day he sold every loaf because it was national bread day doesn't mess up his planning. Nor does the day he only sold three loaves because it was national gluten-free day. As our baker plans, he can become much more accurate when using a standard deviation to give the mean, more meaning.

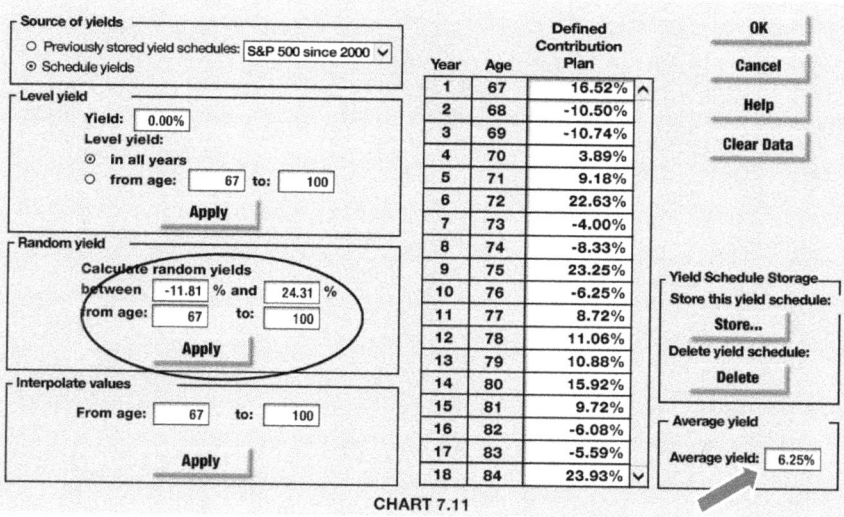

CHART 7.11

The example in chart 7.12 (pg. 93) illustrates how we've eliminated the extremes to hedge our bets. This example uses one standard deviation and an average rate of return of 6.25%. It does also include inflation of 2% and a 22% tax rate. Here's what this looks like

Average Return	Standard Deviation	
6.25%	18.06%	
	Low	High
1	-11.81%	24.31%	66.0%
2	-29.87%	42.37%	30.0%

		Retirement Plan Assets Initial Value 500,000	Retirement Plan Assets Cost Basis 0		Retirement Plan Account Yield See Col. 4	Retirement Income Tax Rate 22.00%	
		(1)	(2)	(3)	(4)	(5) After Tax	(6)
Year	M/F Ages	Beginning of Year Plan Assets	Before Tax Required Minimum Distribution	Before Tax Distribution	Retirement Plan Assets Yield (Avg. 5.53%)	Cash Flow from Retirement Plan Assets	Year End Retirement Plan Assets
1	67/67	500,000	0	32,051	16.52%	25,000	538,439
2	68/68	538,439	0	32,692	10.50%	25,500	551,865
3	69/69	551,865	0	33,346	-10.74%	26,010	457,045
4	70/70	457,045	0	34,013	3.89%	26,530	433,994
5	71/71	433,994	0	34,694	-9.18%	27,061	358,111
6	72/72	358,111	0	35,387	22.63%	27,602	390,809
7	73/73	390,809	14,748	36,095	-4.00%	28,154	336,269
8	74/74	336,269	13,187	36,817	-8.33%	28,717	271,076
9	75/75	271,076	11,019	37,553	23.25%	28,291	284,219
10	76/76	284,219	11,992	38,304	-6.25%	29,877	227,664
11	77/77	227,664	9,942	39,071	8.72%	30,475	202,475
12	78/78	202,475	9,203	39,851	11.06%	31,084	178,353
13	79/79	178,353	8,453	40,649	10.88%	31,706	150,778
14	80/80	150,778	7,464	41,462	15.92%	32,340	125,135
15	81/81	125,135	6,450	42,291	9.72%	32,987	89,760
16	82/82	89,760	4,852	43,137	-6.08%	33,647	43,241
17	83/83	43,241	2,443	43,241	0.00%	33,728	0
18	84/84	0	0	0	0.00%	0	0
19	85/85	0	0	0	0.00%	0	0
20	86/86	0	0	0	0.00%	0	0

Chart 7.12

in chart 7.12. Here, the results are better than the market returns with the slow start we've shown previously, however getting better returns is only part of the equation.

I started this chapter with the story of The Wizard of Oz, and, of course, the yellow brick road metaphor. All the numbers are examples of how important it is to make sure that the assumptions going into your retirement plan are reasonable and, more importantly, believable as well!

The Get Me to Zero strategy is designed to help you determine a course of action that helps you sleep at night, knowing you've done all you can to remove the variables from your retirement strategy BEFORE you get to retirement.

The only thing that is beyond our control, in most examples, is inflation. Inflation is a devaluation of currency whereby you have more money chasing fewer products or services. Imagine a lifetime in retirement where you're not worrying about how inflation could raise your taxes! Raise your taxes? Well, of course, if you need to NET a higher and higher amount of income because of inflation, and all your assets are fully taxable, it requires you to "gross up" your withdrawal by a higher and higher amount. As you can see, where we have shown inflation in our examples, the "before tax distribution" goes higher and higher, which inflates your tax liability. It's an ugly mess, isn't it?

At the back of the book, you will see some questions to ask your advisor, or a new advisor, in an initial interview that can help you understand how they address these issues.

In my view, the most important point as you are preparing for retirement is to consider how far above zero you can be in taxes and survive. How much over zero risk do you need to take to get you the potential returns necessary to meet your income objectives, and God forbid, how much of your retirement income do you need to service debt? Zero becomes a powerful number. As you start your voyage on that Yellow Brick Road to retirement, staying focused on the three zeros might just be simple enough to help you create the retirement you've always dreamed of.

Retirement income planning is a mosaic of compounding variables. Many excellent retirement specialists can and do model results using the mix of assets you own. The problem is that neither the client nor the advisor seems to approach the planning with more than a few recommendations for investments, insurance, beneficiary planning and so forth.

I think it is finally time to make sure that both you and your advisor know that the goal is to get you to zero debt (as fast as possible), and by the time you retire, zero, or as close to zero as possible income taxes, and zero risk on your distribution assets for income. That doesn't mean that along the way you don't invest, but before doing so, it is imperative that you get out of debt and that you have a significant savings component in your plan. In the next chapter, I will make some suggestions on how to save and why.

Chapter Eight

I Didn't Know That I Didn't Know That.....

Look at the chart below. The circle represents four very important things:

☐ What I know.

☐ What I know I don't know.

☐ What I think I know that isn't so

☐ What I don't know I don't know

What I know:

First, there are things I know, and I know I know them, and they are truisms. For example, I know that if I want good health;

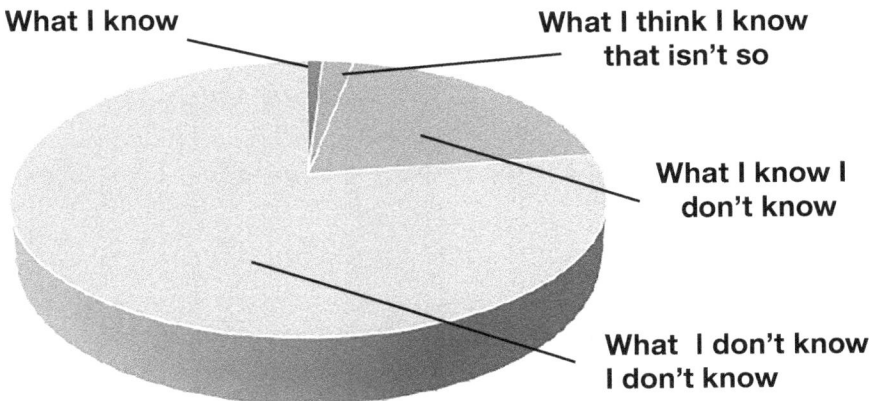

I need to eat well, exercise regularly, work on my emotional well-being and in my case have faith in God. I know for sure that when I do these things; I feel better physically, emotionally, and spiritually.

I also know that $2 + 2 = 4$. I know my car runs well when I take care of it. I know my wife is my very best friend. When I think of these things, however, I understand that what I know is the tiniest fraction of all the knowledge in the universe! I may give myself too big a slice of this pie for the stuff I know I Know!

What I know I don't know:

I also know a wealth of information about my professional field, but I don't know everything. The difference here is that I know where and how to find the answers to the things I need to know. I also know how to double check the answers I find. That's almost as good as knowing it all, but perhaps it's more important to be able to research what I need. My dentist is a doctor, but that doesn't mean he can take my appendix out!

There are millions of things however, I know I don't know. For example, I have never once in my life changed the oil in my cars. I drive a Lexus RX 350 and I would be hard pressed to even find the dipstick for the oil. Now, for all you macho men out there who think, "what kind of man doesn't know how to change his own oil?' I say, I've never needed to know. I go to one of the quick oil change stops in my area and I let someone who does know, do that for me. I don't know how to do it. I know I don't know how to do it. And I don't care. I never have.

But the same folks who would laugh at me for not knowing how to change my oil might not be able to play the most magnificent musical instrument ever invented; the pipe organ in a large church. That I DO know how to do. Even though I've never changed the oil in my car, I'm going to bet it doesn't take as long to learn how to do that as it does to know what to do when you sit down at a set of 5 keyboards and foot pedals to play a composition written by the masters. One is not better than the other, and I would argue all day that the world needs oil changing guys more than it needs organists. But nonetheless, we all have various talents and different degrees of knowledge about different things. In fact, the great American philosopher Will Rogers once said, "Everybody is ignorant, just on different subjects." Truer words were never spoken.

What I don't know I don't know:

The largest piece of the knowledge pie is for stuff that I don't even know that I don't know. This section of the pie is the largest for just about every human being that has ever lived, but we don't think about it because it's nonexistent to us. When this knowledge comes to us, it's usually exciting, invigorating, mind expanding. And unfortunately, sometimes the new knowledge is embarrassing or even frightening. In either case, new knowledge is essential for our continued growth as humans.

What I think I know, that just ain't so:

Without a doubt, the piece of the pie that gets me (and most of us) in trouble the most, and after 43 years in the financial industry where I've heard it all, is the stuff we think we know, that just ain't so. In other words, we might have an opinion about something that is based upon completely erroneous or false information, but we think it is true. When it comes to financial knowledge, this is where trouble comes. In almost every situation where someone states an opinion as fact, I find it difficult, if not impossible, to help them understand why they are wrong when they are. The question here is, "If what you knew to be true, turned out not to be true, when would you like to know?" Probably yesterday. And this, my friends, is where Karma comes to life.

When we act on something based upon opinions, or worse yet, fail to make what would be a significant decision based upon opinions, we often create Karmic debt in our financial life. This falls into my category of making poor financial decisions in my personal life. I am the first to admit, if there's a financial mistake, I've probably made it. I've bought homes I shouldn't have. I leased a car based on how my former CPA shared his opinion that it was a smart move for me. I now despise car leases based on that experience! In my opinion, it's absolutely the worst way to drive a car and I will never be convinced otherwise. The important thing, however, is that I am speaking from experience. In fact, you will ALWAYS have a car payment when you lease! Talk about financial jail! (Yet, some of you will swear by leasing based on your experience and opinion, but I admit, you likely have different goals than I do.)

Another example of how "what I knew that just weren't true" led me to a huge financial mistake where I canceled a very good whole life policy I purchased when I was 26 because I thought I should "Buy term and invest the difference." Yup, I fell into that trap too! Had I kept it (I still have the original illustrations), the cash value when I turned 65 last year was projected to be $198,000. Man, I would love to have that policy in force today. And now in my 60s when I need and want life insurance, and lots of it so that the love of my life won't have to worry if I die first, I had to convert a very large term policy for a very large premium so that the policy wouldn't die before I did. Again, you get my opinion, life insurance is a MUST HAVE if you are married in retirement. That is without exception. I will have more to say about this later.

When we are honest about how we approach our financial decisions, we usually find that much of what we believe to be true is in fact not true and is based upon partial information or, even worse, someone else's opinion. The old saying is don't discuss politics or religion in a social setting. I strongly encourage that financial opinions be included in the off-limits discussions as well. I've had many folks share their "knowledge" about financial issues that were clearly nothing more than strong opinions, and usually, they borrowed someone else's opinion to have as their own.

The little three letter word why is powerful when someone gives me an opinion but calls it a fact. Usually, the reasons for their opinion are based upon someone else's experience, such as their mom, or dad, or uncle, or friend, who said they had a "bad experience" which they gloriously expound upon at length. For example, I may have someone say, "I hate life insurance!" My first reaction is to simply ask, "Why?" Usually, it is because of someone else's opinion or explanation of how life insurance works. Understanding why you feel a certain way about anything, let alone financial issues, is always a good idea. Often, when we self-examine our motives, it is an opportunity to learn.

Let me be direct. My philosophy of getting to zero is not something I've always believed to be the priority in financial planning. In fact, I only recently changed my opinion on paying off your primary residence. For the last 16 years I've focused solely on retirement income planning. Having met with hundreds of people over these years, the happiest, most confident, most relaxed people I ever meet are those who are completely debt free, have no money at risk, or if they do, they are not concerned about losing it, and who pay little to no income tax at all. Ironically, often the most stressed and worried people are those with sufficient money but won't spend a nickel for fear of losing it.

I've learned that financial peace of mind doesn't come from having a lot of money, it comes from not having money problems. That's why I am now passionately focused on helping people focus on getting to ZERO. I now believe that there is no greater service I can provide as a financial coach than this. There are of course, a class of the very wealthy who don't care about debt, or taxes, or risk at all. I did not write this book for them. It is intended to help folks who want to smartly prioritize their finances as they get older.

Let's look at each ZERO one more time and discuss how you can accomplish this goal. First, let's start with getting to ZERO debt.

Zero Debt

The universe works in mysterious ways. As I was preparing to work on writing this chapter, I read a news story about a young woman who got out of $71,000 of debt in just two years by doing what is called "cash stuffing." Simply put, this is where you step back in time to a technique your grandparents, maybe even your parents used. They set up envelopes for each budget item. They deposited cash into each envelope, and that's all they could spend on each budget item. This young woman from the news story is now turning her success into a business. That's fabulous! I wish her luck. Using her system, she will help so many people who desperately need it. I fear, however, that if we ever go to a digital currency; this method will be in big trouble. There's a lot to like about this method and I commend her on doing something fantastic and sharing it with others!

I also must give credit to Dave Ramsey, who, while I believe him to be uninformed about certain aspects of finance for which he has very strong opinions, has taught thousands of people how to get out of debt. Remember, though, Dave talks about having to go bankrupt himself to get out of debt. Dave also is allowed to give all kinds of financial opinions for which he is not properly licensed to provide because he is an "entertainer." The problem I've always had with financial celebrities is that so often their advice is not advice at all, it's opinion—opinions which are wrong on several fronts, particularly regarding life insurance and its amazing utility and tax benefits. Yet, in Dave's case, he has helped lots of people get out of debt. Kudos!

The only problem with many of the get-debt-free systems is once you devote all your finances to paying off debt, you're out of money too! I met an advisor at a conference recently who told me he went through Dave's program and yes; he got out of debt. The problem was, by the time he got there, he desperately needed a car and because he did not save while paying off his debt, he went right back into debt to buy the car. He is now an advisor in the unique Debt Free 4 Life™ program, which uses whole life as a savings vehicle to both save, protect, and pay off debt. There is a similar system known as EquityXL™ which is almost a clone of the Debt Free 4 Life™ system.

Yes, I have opinions too. Opinions shaped by experience in the retirement income planning space.

While the Debt Free 4 Life™ system or the Equity XL™ system of becoming debt free often takes a little longer because they encourage the use of a properly designed whole life policy, I love the end results because once you're debt free, you also have accumulated cash values in your life insurance policy that you might be able to collateralize for the purchase of that car or some other major purchase.

Here's how collateralization of a life policy works.

Most whole life policies have a fixed loan rate built into them. This is the rate at which you can borrow money from the life insurance company using your policy cash values as collateral. The insurance company doesn't care what the money is for. There is no credit check and no reporting to a credit agency on your payments, and they don't even care if you pay it back! If you don't pay it back, they simply deduct any outstanding loans from your death benefit. But even that's a bonus because you won't be leaving any debt to your family if that happened. But what if the rates at the bank are even better than your policy loan rate? Often, you can pledge the appropriate cash values as collateral to the bank and in many cases can borrow from them at a better rate. The point is that when you reduce your "debt service" payments, you gain financial strength and, more importantly, financial confidence grows along with it. The caution here is that paying off your debt and getting to zero should never mean that you're free to start over and take on more debt. How many times have I seen someone pay off a car loan, and then in the next few months, they're at it again with another one!

This requires some humility and reflection. I marvel at how so many of us buy things we don't need, with money we don't have, to impress people we don't know. Cars are at the very top of that list. If you are killing yourself with high payments to drive a car that you really know is out of your budget, the question is why? Even If you have the coolest wheels anywhere, trust me, people will look at the car, but most of them don't care who's driving it. For some people, the car they drive is very important. I switched from being one of the aforementioned to bragging about how many miles I plan to drive my current car.

As I write this, I'm driving a 7-year-old Lexus RX 350 with 112,000 miles on it. It runs great. I think I have at least another 100,000 miles to go! My last car, which was the car my FORMER CPA advised me to lease, and which I purchased at the end of the lease, was a Toyota Avalon that had 216,000 miles on it when I gave it to my mother. It still drove like the day I got it and when she passed away, I sold it for much more than the typical 13-year-old car price. I felt a whole different kind of pride over that. But it was an expensive lesson. I paid for that car twice! But I learned my lesson. Never again will I lease a car. Take note as you see automobile ads; they seldom focus on price—they focus on payments. Hmmm.

Getting out of debt is the first order of business. If you use credit cards to pay your bills and find that your balance is growing every month, then obviously there's a problem. The first thing to do is to list every bill and the minimum payments necessary. Then look at how much you pay on each bill. A minimum payment for a credit card, or most other debts, gets eaten up in interest and fees. Progress is slow going.

Permit me here to summarize why the use of a program like Debt Free 4 Life™ or Equity XL™ differs from how other debt elimination programs work, and why it's an important part of the thinking behind the Get Me to Zero strategy. The popular debt payoff method known as the "debt snowball" works with the idea that you make your minimum payment on all your debts and put any extra funds towards your smallest debt. Once the smallest debt is paid off, you "snowball" that payment and extra funds towards the next smallest debt. As you pay each debt off, the size of your "extra payments' gets bigger and bigger, until your snowball becomes an avalanche bearing down on your largest debt (usually a mortgage). In theory, this is a great idea. You pay off your debts much faster and save a ton of interest. I said "in theory" and yes, it is a proven theory, but what happens once you pay all your debts? Most commonly, you have no money saved and if you need to make any sizable purchase, you do it once again, with debt!

There are many ways to research how to eliminate your debt. I would like to acknowledge the kindness of Dr. Jon Wittwer, creator of the Vertex calculators online, who graciously has allowed me to direct you to his free online debt elimination software. You can find it here; https://www.vertex42.com/Calculators/debt-reduction-calculator.html. For you do-it-yourselfers who just want to download a calculator to help you with this, I highly recommend this software. But I believe that this strategy requires much more than your own self discipline to follow Dr. Wittwer's excellent software. That's why I wrote this book! A good Get Me to Zero advisor will likely encourage you to attack the elimination of debt using more than a calculator, but this is an excellent place to start!

This is where the Get Me to Zero and the use of a life insurance component rises above all other debt management plans. Consider the use of life insurance in your strategy to be a piece of the Get Me to Zero system as a modified snowball. It's a matter of utilizing the "extra" payments more strategically. Instead of attacking your smallest debt, your extra funds instead go into a special compound interest account (let's call this your financial confidence account). So instead of paying interest, you're now collecting it! Then when you have enough funds (with some additional savings built-in), you pay off that smallest debt in full.

Now, the minimum payments you were making towards that debt also go into your financial confidence account. When it's time to pay off the next debt, you can pay it in full out of your account, without completely draining it. With this process, you pay off your debt nearly as fast, but in the end, you're not sitting on zero dollars in your bank account. You have a savings account with tens (or even hundreds) of thousands of dollars in it. You may never need to take a loan for any big purchase ever again. Instead, you simply borrow from yourself.

The use of life insurance systems such as EquityXL™ or Debt Free 4 Life™ I mentioned, and which I endorse wholeheartedly, is, in my opinion, the best way to tackle debt. I will not get into all the details here, but you can visit this website to learn more. www.

GetMetoZerodebt.com. Before we leave the debt discussion, let me just emphasize one more time why this is the starting point.

When you owe a debt and make a payment, let's say of $500 towards the balance, that $500 is gone forever. You not only have that $500 permanently leave your personal economy, so has all the interest or growth you could have earned on that money if it were saved or invested. That's called lost opportunity cost. Besides forever having that money and the lost earnings disappear from your personal economy, as I stated in chapter 2, most of us spend about 34% of our income each month on interest payments! Getting rid of that, especially in a plan that also helps you develop a plan for the other two zeros down the road, is a tremendous relief. You recover back to yourself further lost opportunity costs and the actual money.

In our Get Me to Zero planning process, we use one of the systems mentioned here for the debt elimination part of the Get Me to Zero strategy, but we don't serve clients everywhere, and we can't handle all the requests. We do, however, have access to several advisors who are passionate about teaching clients how to get out of debt. We will point you in the right direction.

As I mentioned earlier, I strongly believe that it is important, especially in today's financial environment, to pay off your mortgage. The only exception to that is if you're not sure that you are living in your last house. But even if you're not living in your last house, paying off all your other debt and then super funding your life insurance policy will give you a lot more financial fire power when it comes time to purchase the next house. The combination of equity rolling from your current house to the next, coupled with a hefty policy cash value, will put you in a dominant position to get into the next home and pay it off sooner rather than later.

One final thought about paying off the mortgage. I used to be one of the biggest proponents of NOT paying off the mortgage, especially when the interest rates were so low. No sense paying off a debt with a 3% loan rate when you could invest the money you would use for that to make a higher rate of return. Right? Here's why I have changed my mind. In today's economy, I believe that owning assets, like a home and yes like a life insurance policy is very important due to the coming uncertainty we are likely to see as the world economy moves into what I believe will be a more unified global economy. A new currency could replace our dollar very soon. The stock market and other ways to invest could change dramatically in the coming years. Owning a home outright as an asset will in my opinion be more meaningful than ever in these circumstances. It is also a huge boost to one's economic confidence. It's the last debt to pay off, but now, I believe it is necessary.

So, the first Get Me to Zero "how to" is to find a debt elimination plan and stick to it. This is hard. But it is necessary to eliminate debt first.

Now, Let's Talk About Zero Income Taxes

While you are employed and earning income, you must report your income to the IRS and pay taxes on that income. If you are lucky enough to have a pension when you retire, depending upon the amount, you will probably have to pay taxes on it, and it will also likely cause some of your Social Security to become taxable income as well. There may be a workaround, however!

Many pensions also have a lump sum option. For many reasons, this might be a superb choice for you. It requires careful analysis and thought. Most advisors love lump sum rollovers from pension plans. There are many reasons that this may be your best option. One of these reasons might be that you could roll your lump sum into an IRA account and then slowly convert it to a tax-free Roth. Remember, when you convert to a Roth, you owe taxes on the conversion amount. Whether you have a plan to come up with the tax money on that conversion amount will greatly affect whether it makes sense to do so.

Here is where and why using life insurance in your debt elimination system can be so helpful and impact your ability to facilitate a Roth conversion. Chart 8.1 offers a look at the Roth conversion section of our software. I always want to make sure that the conversion makes sense before I coach a client to take the lump sum pension.

Chart 8.1 (pg. 105) helps us find out whether we can consider a Roth.

First, the top left section says there are three scenarios:

1.   The client already has a Roth.

Roth defined contribution plan for Valued Client

Roth Status
- Client has a current Roth
- ⊙ Client does not have a current Roth but intends to convert an existing Defined Contribution plan to a Roth
- Client has a current Roth and intends to convert an existing Defined Contribution plan to a Roth

Yield
- ⊙ Yield: 0.00 %   Use a 2nd yield: 0.00 %   Starting at age: 67
- Schedule...   yields
- Stored schedules: ____ ▾   Review

Withdraw funds:
- ⊙ as needed (use like any other liquid asset)
- per schedule Schedule...   thereafter as needed
- per schedule Schedule...   and for no other purpose
- using level after tax distributions that deplete the account
  - over 0 year (s), starting at age 67

Penalty Tax Settings...

Schedule Roth Conversion

Conversion details: Schedule...

The source of the funds for the income tax due on the Roth conversion can be selected on the "Schedule" screen

Account data

Client age when current Roth was established: 62

Current value: $0   Remaining cost basis: $0

- Schedule additional contributions: Schedule...

Roth management fee: 0.0000 %

Charitable bequests

- Include Charitable Bequests at age: 67
- ⊙ 100.00 % of retirement plan asset value
- Up to $0 in value

Change All...

CHART 8.1

2.   The client does not have a Roth but is intending to convert an existing defined contribution plan (this can be 401(k), IRA, 403(b), or 457) to a Roth.

3.   The client has a Roth and intends to roll the plan or convert it into their existing Roth.

The box to the right asks us what the conversion schedule is going to be. I've had clients tell me their advisor talked them out of a conversion because of the restrictive tax liability. They were not aware that you do not have to convert all at once! There is other information on this page of the software that we must consider as well, such as account data, when we intend to withdraw money from the Roth or even if we intend to add additional funds to it after we have it. We also need to consider where to invest the funds. Please note, we are simply moving beyond opinions (even my opinions) and looking at data to shape our decisions.

The next thing we must consider is the conversion schedule. This is where we will probably say yeah or nay to the conversion.

Here is where it gets real.

On the top of chart 8.2 (pg. 106), we enter an amount we intend to convert, and on what schedule. Sometimes people want to convert a little more each year, thus the growth rate. The box in the top middle, however, is where we ask the most important question.

Change Roth IRA Conversion Income Tax Rate

Change level amount

Level amount: ____ $0

⊙ in all years

○ from age: 67 to: 100

Apply   ⊙ to col 2
          ○ to col 4

Change growth rate

Rate: 0.00 %

⊙ Use a second rate of 0.00 %

Starting at age: 67

Apply   ⊙ to col 2
          ○ to col 4

Interpolate values

From age: 67 to: 100

Apply   ⊙ to col 2
          ○ to col 4

Level depletion

Level amount that depletes the account over 1 years starting at age: 67

Apply

Income tax on Roth IRA conversion
○ Let the system figure it out
⊙ I'll specify the amount

Source of funds for the income tax on the Roth Conversion:
⊙ Any excess cash flow followed by my liquid assets based on the prioritization established under the Prioritize the Use of Assets sub-tab available under the Illustration Details tab.
○ The following liquid asset: [Roth Defined Contr. (Valued Client) @ 0.00% ▾]

Change Roth IRA Conversion Income Tax Rate

Year	Ages	(1) Value of Account (After Required Min. Distr.)	(2) Conversion Amount	(3) Conversion Amount Including 0.00% Growth	(4) Income Tax on Conversion	(5) End of Year Value in Account
1	67/67	500,000	0	0	0	519,500
2	68/68	519,500	0	0	0	539,761
3	69/69	539,761	0	0	0	560,812
4	70/70	580.812	0	0	0	582,694
5	71/71	582,684	0	0	0	605,409
6	72/72	605,409	0	0	0	629,020
7	73/73	605,283	0	0	0	628,889
8	74/74	604,277	0	0	0	627,792
9	75/75	602,272	0	0	0	625,761
10	76/76	599,358	0	0	0	622,733
11	77/77	595,539	0	0	0	618,765

OK

Cancel

Help

Clear Data

CHART 8.2

How are we going to pay the tax on the conversion?

You notice we can plan the tax amount we need, and we can tell the system we have the funds somewhere else in the plan to come up with the taxes, or we can deduct them from the conversion amount. (I never recommend a conversion if that's the way we're going to handle the taxes). In this example, I simply show the money coming from "excess cash flow." Now let's stop and think for a moment. If we convert to the Roth after all we paid the debt, then it follows that we can use all the increased cash flow created because you no longer have debt payments. If you've chosen the life insurance option as part of your debt elimination strategy, we encourage you to continue your life insurance premiums as a SAVINGS instrument. If you're converting the IRA over time, you can leverage the cash values in your policy either once a year, or depending upon how long you have to retirement, every other year. When you leverage those taxes via a policy loan, you can recapture the cost by paying off the loan casually over time. This is an extremely powerful way to convert a taxable asset with tax-free income from another "Roth like" asset in your financial arsenal. It's almost like having another Roth to help you convert to a Roth!

Now, your "financial confidence" account serves a second purpose. It can help you to plan for a Roth conversion of some, or preferably all your taxable retirement assets to tax-free Roths or maybe to another specially designed Indexed Universal Life policy built for income. More on this later.

Permit me to insert a brief glossary here before I get all insurance jargony, and you think I'm crazy. Remember, you are not crazy and I don't want you to think I am.

Roth IRA: A Roth IRA is an individual retirement account that offers tax-free growth and tax-free withdrawals in retirement. You fund a Roth IRA with after-tax dollars.

IRA: An IRA is a long-term savings account set up at a financial institution that allows an individual to save for retirement on a tax-deferred basis. Withdrawals are taxable.

Roth Conversion: A Roth conversion is repositioning your assets from a traditional IRA or qualified employer sponsored retirement plan (QRP), such as a 401(k), 403(b), or governmental 457(b) to a Roth IRA. This is done to create tax free income.

IUL: Indexed Universal Life insurance is a type of permanent life insurance, which means it has a cash value component besides a death benefit.

Whole Life: Whole life insurance policies provide permanent life insurance and typically offer fixed premiums, fixed death benefits, and a cash value savings component.

HELOC: A Home Equity Line of Credit is a line of credit secured by your home that gives you a revolving credit line to use for large expenses or to consolidate higher-interest rate debt on other loans such as credit cards.

HECM: The only reverse mortgage insured by the U.S. Federal Government is called a Home Equity Conversion Mortgage (HECM), and is only available through an FHA-approved lender. The HECM is FHA's reverse mortgage program that enables you to withdraw a portion of your home's equity.

GMTZ – Get Me to Zero – The three-phase strategy to eliminate debt, minimize the tax burden to as close to Zero as possible, and bring your retirement money to zero risk.

LIFO vs. FIFO

While LIFO is an acronym for last-in, first-out, FIFO stands for first-in, first-out. The LIFO method is based on the idea that the most recent products in your inventory will be sold first. The FIFO method is the opposite as it assumes the oldest products in your inventory will be sold first and uses those lower cost numbers when calculating tax liabilities on withdrawals.

MYGA: A Multi-Year Guaranteed Annuity, or MYGA, is a type of fixed annuity that offers a guaranteed fixed interest rate for a certain period, usually from three to 10 years. A MYGA is often appropriate for someone who is closer to retirement and prefers tax deferral and a guarantee of investment return.

SPIA: A Single Premium Immediate Annuity is an annuity purchased with one large upfront payment. The SPIA immediately begins paying you back your purchase price plus a modest interest rate in installments.

FIA: A Fixed Index Annuity is an insurance contract that provides you with income in retirement. With a Fixed Index Annuity, payments are based on the performance of a stock market index, like the S&P 500. Unlike owning stocks, you're protected against most losses—but your total returns may also be limited.

Here's some information about the Roth retirement accounts.

Let's start with a little secret. You may know that you must let a Roth rest for 5 years before you can pull any of the interest out tax free. You can start a Roth at your bank for $100.00 and that establishes the date of your Roth! I advise clients all the time to start a Roth years before the intended conversion so that the 5 years are past. New contributions and earnings do NOT start a new 5 year wait.

There is also some misunderstanding that you can't have a Roth if your income exceeds certain thresholds. That rule does NOT apply to Roth conversions. Conversions are not subject to the income qualification rules!

Once you've converted your IRA accounts to Roth accounts, have recaptured all the tax loans if you leveraged your life insurance policy to do so, you now have two sources of tax-free income when you retire!

Roth accounts, and life insurance loans or basis withdrawals are the two easiest ways to design tax-free income in retirement. You can review whether you want to go further and consider a HECM. If this is all done correctly, I think you will be fine without one, but remember, with the GMTZ strategy paying off debt first, including your house, is key. If you owe nothing on your house, then I think having a HELOC (home equity line of credit) is a good idea, even if you never use it. You only pay interest on an outstanding balance, otherwise it's an emergency fund if you need it. You can always consider rolling any HELOC balances, if any, into a HECM later in life.

One last thought about the whole life policy you will need if you choose the Get Me to Zero and life insurance strategy. Be sure that you are buying the life insurance policy from a company that is financially sound. I recommend that you only buy this policy from a mutual life insurance company and make sure that you know all about the insurance company's solvency before choosing to work with that company.

This GMTZ insurance policy needs to be designed properly. A good advisor in either the EquityXL™ system or the Debt Free 4 Life ™ system is going to voluntarily take a substantial cut in the commissions they could earn if they simply wrote a standard policy. Instead, the system is designed to have your premiums divided into a "base" policy, which typically will encompass about 50% to 60% of the premium you pay. The balance is then used to purchase additional paid-up insurance, which supercharges the cash values. Your advisor makes substantially fewer commissions by doing this, but it is in your best interest, and they are more than happy to do it.

Zero Risk

I already spent a chapter explaining why you may want ZERO risk to your INCOME-producing assets in retirement. I see the only way to guarantee that is by using fixed or fixed indexed annuities. Annuities have been around since the Roman Empire in one form or another, but in the United States they were first used to create pension incomes for Presbyterian ministers. They were also used after the Civil War in the US to help widows of deceased soldiers. They are the basis for every single pension plan. Even if the plan doesn't use an actual annuity, they call your lifetime pension payments annuities.

Annuities, however, have a poor reputation among some in the financial world. That is because of three main reasons.

First, many people think all annuities are like the old single premium annuities whereby you paid a premium to the annuity company in return for income. If you died before you got all your income back, the company kept the balance. This is where you can easily be fooled by someone else's experience. Old annuities worked that way, and "life only" income options still work that way. The best way to understand this is that many folks who are deciding on which option to take if they are selecting pension income, understand that if they have no survivors for their income, it will be much higher. When selecting a pension option, married individuals are required to have their spouses sign off on their selected option. If they elect a life only pension option and die even after the first check, their survivors receive nothing. This is how many old annuities were designed. Today, all income annuities have survivor options. There are countless settlement options for annuities that assure that this doesn't happen. This is one of those danger zones where opinions are based on erroneous facts!

Second, many people purchased annuities that did NOT remove market risk. They are called Variable Annuities. Chart 8.3 shows where we insert the details for annuities in our software. Variable annuities require the section in the black box to be completed. Other fixed annuities do not have these charges and fees.

Here in Chart 8.3, you see that we must account for the various charges and fees in the variable annuities. Here is why I dislike them. There are simply too many! Whatever the total of these

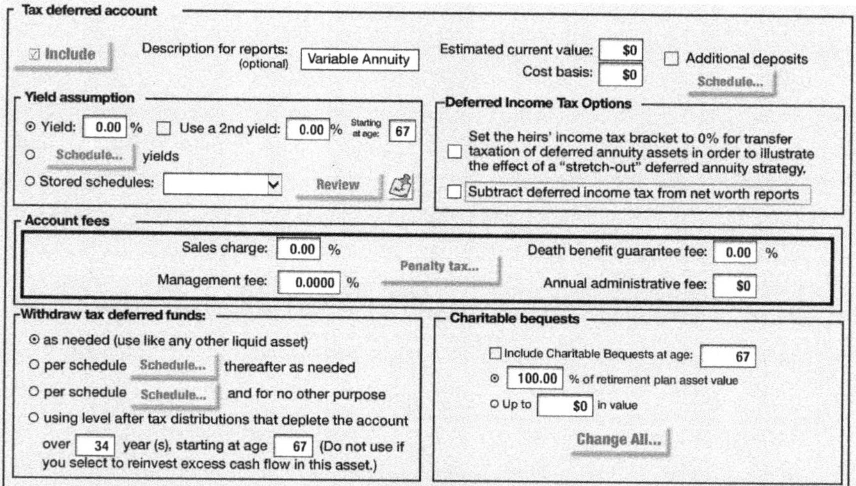

CHART 8.3

fees and charges add up to, is the deductible on your returns each year. In addition, since these are treated as investments first, they are subject to market risk. But didn't your agent say you got a guaranteed interest rate on your annuity? Yes, they may have told you that, but that is NOT on your premium. It is on the income rider value, which can only be taken as income.

I like income riders since they are designed to ignore investment returns for the income account value, but with almost no exceptions, the clients believe that the actual premium is receiving that guarantee. It's so frustrating. Sometimes my clients even tell me they were assured that they were "guaranteed" X% on their money. It is NOT on the actual premium which had been invested in sub accounts, which are often expensive and poorly performing mutual funds. Variable annuities are exceptional when the market is roaring, but they are highly deficient in a down market. If not variable annuities, then what? Sadly, those that I consider to be the best type of annuities may not always be attractive. Huh?

That's right, depending upon the interest rates they are paying, the most popular annuities pay fixed interest rates just like a bank account with a few notable exceptions. First, if you place after tax money in an annuity, you defer the taxes on the interest until you withdraw the money. Remember LIFO and FIFO? These are LIFO products UNLESS they are Roth accounts. I LOVE these for Roths! This can be good if you don't need the funds, but not so good if your children are the beneficiaries since the beneficiaries pay the taxes on the inherited interest in an annuity (except for Roths) and it's taxed as ordinary income. For this reason alone, many CPAs pooh-pooh annuities. (it's funny though, these same CPAs are often silent on mutual funds attributable gains where you never got to spend the income you're being taxed on!) The good news once again is that if your children ultimately inherit an annuity, (usually because there is no surviving spouse), your tax-free life insurance death benefit, assuming you purchased life insurance for the debt elimination part of your Get Me to Zero strategy can satisfy that tax liability.

What's great about fixed interest rate annuities? Well, if you didn't skip chapter 6, you know why! Go back to the discussion of fixed interest returns while drawing down income versus market based. Insert the word Multi Year Guaranteed Annuity (MYGA) for the fixed interest side. I like to use what I call the split annuity concept for income. In this strategy, I like to combine what we know as a period certain only single premium annuity, which will pay you or your beneficiary the income for 5 years guaranteed. Live or die, someone gets the money for 5 years (or the balance of 5 years if you die in year two, for example) and a deferred annuity for the remaining balance. This strategy only works well if the interest rates for the MYGAs are at least 3 to 5 percent or higher, of course. The idea is that you split a sum of money into two buckets, one for income, one for deferral, and then you keep cycling it repeatedly.

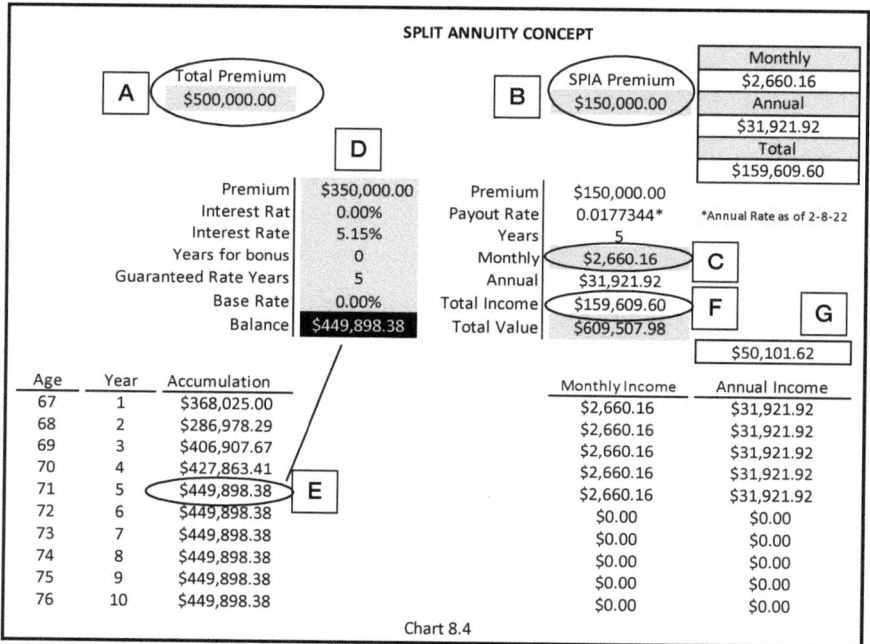

SPLIT ANNUITY CONCEPT

A	Total Premium	$500,000.00

B	SPIA Premium	$150,000.00

	Monthly
	$2,660.16
	Annual
	$31,921.92
	Total
	$159,609.60

D

Premium	$350,000.00
Interest Rat	0.00%
Interest Rate	5.15%
Years for bonus	0
Guaranteed Rate Years	5
Base Rate	0.00%
Balance	$449,898.38

Premium	$150,000.00	
Payout Rate	0.0177344*	*Annual Rate as of 2-8-22
Years	5	
Monthly	$2,660.16	C
Annual	$31,921.92	
Total Income	$159,609.60	F
Total Value	$609,507.98	

G

$50,101.62

Age	Year	Accumulation		Monthly Income	Annual Income
67	1	$368,025.00		$2,660.16	$31,921.92
68	2	$286,978.29		$2,660.16	$31,921.92
69	3	$406,907.67		$2,660.16	$31,921.92
70	4	$427,863.41		$2,660.16	$31,921.92
71	5	$449,898.38	E	$2,660.16	$31,921.92
72	6	$449,898.38		$0.00	$0.00
73	7	$449,898.38		$0.00	$0.00
74	8	$449,898.38		$0.00	$0.00
75	9	$449,898.38		$0.00	$0.00
76	10	$449,898.38		$0.00	$0.00

Chart 8.4

This example, in chart 8.4 shows what that looks like.

- The starting balance is $500,000. (A)

- $150,000 is placed in a 5-year period certain SPIA (B)

- The SPIA pays monthly income of $2,660.16 (C)

- The remaining balance is placed in a 5-year MYGA (D)

- With the interest rate of 5.15%, the $350,000 is guaranteed to grow to $449,898.38 (E)

- Total Income paid to client over 5 years is $159,609.60 (F)

- After 5 years, the client has $50,101.62 less than he started with (G)

So, for a reduction in value from the original amount of $500,000 of just over $50,000 our client has received more than $159,609 of total income. Along with that, in this scenario, they have a balance of $449,898 and they are now 5 years older. We depleted their ORIGINAL amount by just over $50,000 to get all that income. What could we do next? We can do it again! If the client needs more income, we can increase the amount that goes into the next SPIA. If some other way of getting income is more desirable after the 5-year period, there are no longer surrender charges on the MYGA. It can be rolled over to something else with no penalties!

This looks much more complicated than it is. I love this strategy!

Finally, there is another extremely popular annuity product known as fixed indexed annuities (FIAs). These products are much more complicated than above; however they are a kind of Goldilocks alternative to the market based and risky variable annuities, and the more limited MYGAs. They are also longer-term income solutions. Many of them have riders, and there are a few excellent products that do not. While they also are often heavily criticized, particularly by money managers, there are many financial giants like Dr. David Babbel, a professor at the Wharton School of Finance, and Roger Ibbotson who is a well-known expert on markets, and who has a firm that manages a popular index used in a FIA product who find these products to serve well as a bond alternative, perhaps. The General Accounting Office (GAO) annuity.pdf (annuity-insurers.org) has also promoted the use of annuities to secure retirement. The opponents claim to be smarter than the annuity actuaries. Believe me, they're not. Every year, billions of dollars flow into annuities. Is everyone wrong?

Essentially, these FIA annuities offer a way to take part in the growth of specific market indexes over a period, usually one year, but to get a better potential return over as many as 5 years. To give you all the details and possibilities of every indexed annuity here would be prohibitive.

FIAs usually have a rider option as well, like the ones found in many variable annuity contracts, and they are usually available for slightly lower fees than the variable annuities. Some consumer groups think the 3% to 4% commission on the above split annuity solution is too high. They do not deduct it from your premium, but it is a primary reason for lengthy surrender charges. The question is, is it too high? That's a subjective opinion. If they compensate real estate salespeople at an average of 6% to sell a house, it is because real estate is a complex transaction and you need a pro to help you through it. Understanding fixed indexed annuities is equally complex. But here's where the consumer groups miss the boat. No matter where the funds used to purchase an indexed annuity otherwise would reside, there are going to be fees and charges. This compensation allows for an advisor to get paid, but that money should never be subjected to any other ongoing advisory fees.

In comparison then, the annuity agent gets paid, but perhaps the money would have otherwise been in a brokerage account subject to deductible advisory fees for as long as it was there! It usually ends up as a wash over the long term. Even if you pay advisory fees, there still is no contractual recourse to any guaranteed results! All fixed annuities come with guarantees. All these, however, are of course subject to the claims paying ability of the insurance company. That's why when you work with an advisor who is recommending an annuity, be sure to start with understanding the solvency of that company.

Finally, and certainly last, but not least, there is another wonderful opportunity to enhance your tax-free income options, protect your family from your premature death, and most times yourself from the costs of a chronic illness with another wonderful insurance contract. We know this as Indexed Universal Life or IUL. IUL policies have become extremely popular, especially for wealthy families and business owners who are looking for alternatives to saving for retirement in a government sponsored plan like an IRA or 401(k) etc. We must again design these policies in your favor so that you can maximize your cash value growth. They are particularly strong as a long-term accumulation vehicle. I have clients who have hundreds of thousands of dollars in IUL cash values!

I'm tempted to go into a long explanation of them here, but I will resist as there are many outstanding books that explain how IULs are best used and why. I refer you to my friend David McKnight's best-selling book, *"The Power of Zero"* for a thorough understanding of how and why IUL is a perfect financial instrument to build tax-free retirement income. I do NOT believe, however, as some may argue, that IUL is the policy to use for the debt elimination part of the Get Me to Zero strategy. That requires whole life insurance. No exceptions.

Should you reach the point of Freetirement, it will be because you have zero debt, zero planned risk, and zero income tax likely in the way you have structured your planning. IUL can be a lynchpin for the tax-free portion of your retirement income. It is well worth the time to compare using IUL as your main retirement savings vehicle vs funding a 401(k) above the company match.

The bottom line here is that by having contractual guarantees built into your GMTZ system, you accomplish the last ZERO objective of zero risk on your income-producing assets.

At the beginning of this chapter, you saw that pie chart with the tiny little slivers of known information. I know now you are better prepared to have a GMTZ conversation with an advisor regarding your desire to get to zero. Expanding your knowledge has hopefully made you a more informed consumer and a believer that by getting to zero debt, zero income taxes, and zero risk on your retirement income-producing assets, you can be "Freetired" in the coming years!

But just in case you are wondering what questions to ask, I'll give you a little help in the next chapter.

Chapter Nine

Don't Should on Me, And I Promise I Won't Should on You...

There is a large investment advisor firm in our area that does a massive amount of radio advertising. Yes, they are "celebrity advisors" in that they have a radio show. They market commentary on talk radio news stations, and so on. One of their commercials says something like "We care about your money and so should you." I've never met these folks; nor know anyone who works with them. I am always struck, however, by the use of the word "should" when discussing someone else's money.

An old friend once told me why he hates the word "should," thus the opening line at the beginning of this chapter. I try to avoid that word. Let me start with this first red flag when seeking or interviewing an advisor. If they couch their recommendations by telling you what you "should" do, I say, run for the hills! I should lose another 30 pounds. I should spend more time playing the piano, I should eat better. We all know these things. Guess what, in your heart, you already know much of what you "should" be doing with your finances. Being handed a "plan" full of "shoulds" is not the best option.

If you have more debt than you would like, you already know you should do something about it. If you are still too scared to take your money out of savings where you get low interest rates of return, you already know that you should look for a better return, if only to keep up with inflation. If you worry about leaving your loved ones without resources, you realize you should have life insurance. I must say, however, that financial recommendations that start with "You should...," SHOULD be a warning sign that the advisor has trouble listening. Even worse, sometimes they use a cookie cutter approach. I know this is pretty basic, and I don't intend to bash other advisors here, but I find this one thing is a huge indicator of who's in charge of what you are going to do with your money, at least in the eyes of the advisor. It's a bee in my bonnet for sure. Can you tell?

At this point, I should include four paragraphs to present my fundamental basis upon which you may begin establishing your personal road to find the right financial advisor to help you execute your individual Get Me to Zero strategy.

1) Finding the right advisor is a simple task because it starts with becoming Debt Free first. It is a tricky task if you want an advisor to help with your investment and other tax planning as well. Therefore, I think it's fine to begin working with a Debt Free 4 Life™ or EquityXL™ program as one of the best options available.

2) I like these two systems because both have a platform with a robust system to monitor your debt situation and prompt you to make the moves and payments exactly when appropriate to keep you on track. Get Me to Zero, has no independent system for that, and if you agree that one of these debt elimination systems is the one you will use, it all starts with getting to zero debt, and can begin as easily as meeting with an advisor in one of those programs. I want to emphasize here that success in getting out of debt, whether you use these programs or not, requires that you be serious about your goal to be debt free. Any system, including this one, will only work if you follow it as designed. Paying down debt means exactly that. You must be able, for example, to "retire" using a card designated for pay off. Paying down a revolving credit card debt means you STOP USING THAT CARD!

3) These debt elimination programs are specifically designed to make the life insurance component work to your maximum benefit. In chapters three and four, I illustrated how the debt elimination designed whole life insurance contract—is a life insurance plan designed to reduce commissions by half of normal by lowering the base part of the insurance plan. It then adds a paid-up additions rider to allow earlier access to your policy's

cash values. In addition, because it's a policy with a vital NON-DIRECT recognition dividend structure, it provides the math and magic of the whole life strategy. Non-Direct recognition dividend structures will allow you to earn dividends on your entire cash value even though you may have an outstanding policy loan. DO NOT USE DIRECT RECOGNITION WHOLE LIFE POLICIES FOR THIS STRATEGY!

4) It's a good bet to believe that debt elimination advisors start with your best interest in mind by the virtue of the way they must design the whole life policy for the system to work properly. I've never heard a single comment from these advisors about how to squeeze more compensation from the plan. These advisors are passionate about helping folks get out of debt, and they come to the table knowing that the compensation is lower on these policies because of the way they must design them. I don't know how many of these advisors are interested in expanding their scope of planning to include asset management nor, if any, want to distract themselves by adding tax planning or long-term care planning or many other financial issues to the mix. That's OK if your first and most pressing need is to get to ZERO debt. However, as important as it is to get to Zero debt first, using the whole life strategy is critical because it facilitates the other two Get Me to Zero objectives as those two objectives rely heavily on the specially designed whole life insurance policy as described.

Once you go beyond the debt elimination part of your Get Me to Zero strategy and determine that now you want to find a financial advisor, planner, coach, or whatever, this is where the challenges begin. It is important to understand first and foremost what you are looking for in the advisor/client relationship.

Now let's get to the way you can find an advisor, learn how they're paid, why they're paid that way, and whether you feel you get your money's worth. If you expect to work with a great advisor and their team; it is only fair that they earn their fee.

Please understand that much of what follows is opinion based, (mine, of course), and you may feel differently than I do about some of this (which is not a bad thing, you're not crazy). Nothing is free, and if it is, it is usually not worth much. You will pay an advisor, one method or another. It makes sense to know what to look for.

Shopping For and Interviewing Advisors

Referrals:

We always enjoy receiving referrals from our clients and we regularly get a fair number of them. I've been in this business for over 43 years, and I have heard every sales training on why and how to ask for referrals, yet, I've always stunk at it. I guess the reason for this is that I think it's awkward for me to expect my clients to feed my pipeline. I believe we do get referrals for some important reasons. Let me share some of them with you. Hopefully, this can help you figure out what you are looking for. We don't pressure, we just present new prospectives.

There is never, and I mean never, a time when I pressure a client to do something that I am recommending. I may stand firm that I see my proposal as the best solution for them, but I never try to "hard close" a client. Nobody enjoys that process, including me. If I make a reasonable presentation of the facts as I see them, the clients will come to their own conclusion if it makes sense to implement the plan. We use great software that starts with an analysis of what we call, "present position." It illustrates what it looks like if you do nothing different from what you're doing now. It shows your present position. We know this as comparative analysis. I want clients to learn how our planning process and our analysis will show how things are likely to go, given the current set of circumstances and assumptions. This is the risk we take when we interview a new prospective client, since a lot of work is involved in gathering data, entering it properly into our planning software, and spitting out the results.

Once this is done, we then make some changes to the formulas, using perhaps a more conservative portfolio or more aggressive portfolio. We also run scenarios where we use risk transference as a key component. In other words, what does this look like if we transfer the longevity risk to an insurance company using annuities, and if so, which one and why? We may look at adding life insurance to help convert inherited IRA and other highly taxable assets at the death of the account owner. Or, maybe we look at the use of life insurance as a hedge for the surviving spouse to replace vacation spending—meaning if you want to live it up a little more in retirement but are afraid of depleting your accounts too fast so that the survivor has trouble getting by.

We think owning life insurance to replace other assets spent for fun while you are enjoying retirement might make some sense. I like to call it the "ticket to spend policy." These are examples of springboards for discussion with our prospective clients. It also involves an analysis of current investments, costs and fees, tax liability, future potential tax liability, and so forth. It really is a compare-and-contrast strategy. We feel this is much more responsible than having our client come in for a follow-up meeting and we say, "OK, here's what you should do."

Therefore, when interviewing advisors, ask if they will start by analyzing what you're already doing so you know if there are issues you haven't considered or are just wondering what the likelihood is that your current plan will succeed. If you're thinking, "I don't have a plan," I remind you that you do, you just have not written it down. I know advisors who shame the clients by calling their existing plan "the no plan, plan." Shame can be an impactful way of influencing someone, but I sincerely think it's unprofessional.

You may start seeking if you have a trusted friend who can refer you to their advisor. Ask multiple friends who they work with. The only caution I have here is for you to understand that just because someone refers you to their advisor, it doesn't mean that they will be right for you. For example, someone could give me a rave review of a particular restaurant, (can you tell I love to eat?), but I might not care for the type of food they like, no matter how good they think it is. The same thing applies here. Don't accept blindly that this is going to be a good fit, but a referral to a friend's advisor is a good place to start.

Real People Answer the Phone

Another reason we get numerous referrals has nothing to do with me. Well, maybe it does, but we do some of the little things that are appreciated as big things. We answer our telephone. We don't have one of those voice mail press one for this or that, unless everyone is on the phone when someone calls. I truly believe that it is just as important, if not more so, that the advisor has a loyal and happy staff. I could not be prouder of my team members. Erin and Amy know all of our clients and their "stories," and they treat each with dignity and respect at all times. More importantly, they are the keys to implementing a plan. They help with every review and do all the service work needed to get beneficiary forms properly in place, finding those old "computer shares," and move them into a new account, facilitate transfers of money into the proper accounts when we begin a new plan, and even complete applications and forms properly (which is one of my biggest challenges—I hate filling out forms).

When you come to a new appointment with an advisor, or when you communicate with their staff, how do you feel? This is an enormous factor since the staff will be highly involved in helping the advisor to make things work in your plan. Do they seem happy? If waiting for your meeting to start, ask them how they enjoy their job, how long they've been there, what do they like best? Believe me, NOBODY interviews the advisor's staff, yet you can learn more about what you will deal with when you talk to people who work with the advisor you're considering. If there is no staff, or the advisor is a solo practitioner who works out of their home, I would be concerned about cyber security, where in the house they keep your files, who has access to them and what happens if the advisor does not outlive you. I'm not suggesting that you not work with solo practitioners who have no staff, but it would be a red flag for me. If you are working with someone for a specific need, such as a focused Debt Free 4 Life™ advisor, I think this is less of a concern. Interview their staff.

Find Out What They Believe

You'll find a list of questions for the advisor at the end of this chapter, but it is important that you know exactly what you are looking for in an advisor/client relationship. In fact, the entire purpose of this book is to help you find an advisor that will get you to zero debt, zero risk, and zero or as close as possible to zero income taxes when you retire. Assuming you believe in this philosophy, and if you're still reading this, I suspect that Get Me to Zero will be your instructions to the advisor! Since they may not have read this book, and since egos are not in short order in the advisor community, some may pooh-pooh this strategy and will try, maybe even successfully, to tell you this is a bunch of nonsense. They have a better way. Heck, maybe they do! Remember however, you will discuss YOUR money, not their money. As I mentioned earlier, if the first approach to your meeting is criticism of your basic beliefs about money (remember nobody's crazy, including you), I would see that as a serious hindrance to working with them. Find out what they believe.

Find out what and how they invest.

You learned about important financial concepts, such as why reverse dollar cost averaging out of the market can be a disaster when you need income and why using something with ZERO risk for your draw-down income makes sense. Ask the advisor what areas of financial advising they focus on? Is it getting better returns? Is it using annuities for everyone and if so, what are their preferred companies and why? You could start asking many detailed questions, such as what they consider a reasonable risk range for moderately conservative clients. Do they use individual stocks and bonds? Do they use pre-planned portfolios? Do they use third-party money managers? (This means that they are either a solicitor for another advisor, or if they manage their own portfolios). Remember, you are looking for an advisor/coach, NOT a stockbroker. There's nothing wrong with stockbrokers, mind you, but you likely won't get much help from them when it comes to the three GMTZ zeros! Find out what and how they invest.

What will you get in exchange for your fees?

What advisors do is not a commodity and one client who pays an advisor a fee of 1% for assets under management might not get the same quality or level of service as his friend who pays his advisor 1.75%. However, it could be the other way around! It's important you understand what you get in return for any fees. It may not affect your decisions but consider how you initially became exposed to the advisor or his team. Did you attend a free dinner seminar? Did you attend a library training event or perhaps a course on financial matters at a local community college? Were you solicited in the mail or online? I can share with you that new client acquisition is one of the largest challenges that advisors face. An advisor's client acquisition methods may help you understand their business practices. There is not a judgment implied here. But you may find marketing practices positive or negative for your particular level of comfort.

Think how you were approached if you didn't initiate the contact. It sometimes concerns me that the fancier the dinner seminar they invited you to, the more likely that they will steer you towards very profitable products or services. Have you ever fed 60 of your closest friends at a Ruth's Chris steakhouse, for example? Learn the fee structure. (I only do dinner workshops for my clients and their guests).

Are They Working in Your Best Interest?

Many advisors today, including me, are considered as "hybrid" advisors. A "hybrid advisor" can help you with both your investments and insurance. Here, if you are working with an advisor on a plan, and that advisor is a fiduciary, it is NOT a breach of fiduciary standards for them to recommend certain financial products whereby they receive a commission. That is compensation paid to the advisor by the insurance company for the sale of an annuity or life insurance policy. This is often a significant source of revenue for the advisor, assuming you purchase those products from them. Before that, however, two things should happen. First, as a fiduciary, it is a conflict of interest for an advisor to recommend something to you that benefits the advisor more than the client. If an advisor suggests an annuity purchase, for example, it must be demonstrably better for your situation than not having the annuity. The recommendation MUST be in YOUR best Interest. This is why, for example, we use the comparison software we use. Remember, I always want to start with where the client is today.

Any recommendations to purchase specific insurance products must show a demonstrable advantage to my client. That is what the comparison will show. In addition, we must inform you that you are free to purchase that annuity wherever you see fit. The advisor can refer you to his or her insurance entity, but must disclose how and to what extent it compensates them. This includes commissions and all other benefits received by the advisor for placing business with a certain company or product. Just because an advisor gets paid commissions for some of their recommendations does not necessarily mean it is only being recommended because of the commission. This is very important to understand. Advisors have no control over the commission levels paid for certain products. What they can control however is not putting every client in the highest commission products.

As an example, if funds that were to be used to purchase a $500,000 annuity were instead left under management at a fee of 1.5%—which is $7,500 PER YEAR—and for simplicity, assuming that there was no growth or loss on it for the 20 years it was under management, the advisor stands to make much more money on that account. Over that time period more than $150,000 is paid to the advisor. They also deducted it from your investments, creating a drag on performance. In comparison, while they don't directly deduct insurance commissions from the premiums you pay for annuities and life insurance products, they are one of the main reasons for surrender charges and some policy fees. The difference is that many advisors get paid a larger up-front commission for the insurance side, but they give up the recurring fee revenue on the other side. If an advisor is trying to build a successful practice that they plan to sell some day, selling commissionable products in lieu of keeping the money in an advisor managed account is not a brilliant business decision.

You should know that there are best-interest consumer laws today designed to monitor abuse in this area. Here is another red flag, and it's a big one. If you already have an annuity and you go to see another advisor who says you should surrender that product and "roll it" into a new one, especially if you are still in the surrender period; that is usually a big no-no! I've had many clients express their surprise when I told them that the annuity they already had, was a good one. We show how canceling it would cost them X$$, yet, if they choose, assuming they become a client, they could request that we become the agent of record so we can service the policy. Rarely does it make sense to cancel one annuity within the surrender charge period. In rare circumstances, it may make sense to replace an old annuity contract with a new one, but only if it is substantially better. If that is a "you should" with no analysis—red flag!

How Advisors Get Paid.

Let's address advisor compensation from my perspective. I have always felt that I'd love to have a practice where I can charge a flat fee, paid by check or with a credit card instead of an advisory fee deducted from my client's account. I would like to work with a limited number of clients in that way, and any product recommendations or investments are treated the same as any other, except that I would not be deducting fees from any account. Commissions would only be paid if the client purchased them from my insurance agency, and would be paid to the writing agent, and NOT to me. The problem I've always had with this is that most people would rather have the fee deducted, (and many never look at their accounts to see what they are paying), and not have another "bill."

The truth is, paying a flat fee to an advisor is a great deal for the client. Since there is no deduction from the portfolio, it avoids the additional drag on returns, and it is NOT performance based. One very large firm advertises that "We do better when our clients do better." They hold this out as a differentiating factor. It isn't. Almost every advisor I know who charges an Asset Under Management fee (AUM), including me, does better when the portfolio does better. Beware of messaging that claims to be different, when in fact it isn't. This same firm also says it "hates annuities, and so SHOULD you!" If you recall the example above, if you purchase a $500,000 annuity from your agent or advisor and they earn a commission of 7% for example, that's $35,000. Yes, that's a lot of money. But if you recall the earlier example and had the account under management for twenty years at 1.25%, which is an educated guess regarding a fee, you're paying $125,000 over that time. If the account goes up over that time, you're paying even more, and if it goes down, you pay a fee anyway, even if you are losing money. Therefore, it is not safe to assume that just because someone earns a commission, they are only thinking about themselves. It's generally a poor business decision to sell an annuity to a client if the advisor wants to have multiple millions of dollars under management just to expand the value of his or her firm, making it appear more attractive to be acquired. An advisor looking to cash out someday by selling his book of business will not be excited about using fixed or fixed indexed annuities. In other words, if an advisor wants to build a massive block of assets under management (AUM), a block of annuity contracts that has no recurring revenue is a losing proposition. Therefore, if you're one of those folks who thinks anyone who works in a meritocracy whereby they do as well as their efforts afford, is automatically not going to act in your best interest, please consider what I have just outlined.

Having said that, if on the other hand, the only solutions involve commissionable products, (except in focused areas like Debt Free 4 Life™, or EquityXL™ where the design of the policy itself cuts commissions drastically to begin with), that is also a red flag.

Designations

As I have mentioned before, I feel like an old country doctor. I have many years of experience in my work, but I am not a Certified Financial Planner (CFP). I completely respect anyone with the ability to do the hard work necessary to complete a course of study to receive a designation. I also understand and respect that for some consumers, this is the most important issue they are concerned about when looking for an advisor.

I know many talented CFP professionals and I know many more very smart and very talented advisors who do not have a CFP designation as well. In my experience, I once had a CFP who worked with our firm. I thought that since this individual was a CFP, I assumed he knew "everything financial" and I treated him that way. Shockingly, however, I learned quickly that this individual did not understand the most basic application of annuities, could not really explain what they were and how they worked, and in fact made several assumptions that were dangerously wrong when discussing them with clients! This individual also had no true understanding of life insurance products, what a modified endowment was, or why it was important to understand the utility of these products.

Of course, this experience does not mean that all CFPs are the same. My point here is that just because someone has a designation, does not mean that they know how to apply the knowledge.

My wife Michelle and I were on a flight where the flight attendants asked if there were medical professionals on board. A passenger collapsed coming out of the forward lavatory. Michelle is now a retired nurse practitioner, but back then, she was still working. She was asleep when they made the announcement. I woke her. She went forward to see if she could help. When she arrived, a surgeon was also arriving and asking for rubber gloves to "treat" the individual who had a small laceration. While this was all going on, Michelle evaluated the man and learned that he had not eaten breakfast, was likely severely dehydrated and perhaps had low blood sugar and had likely fainted. She mentioned this to the surgeon, and he acknowledged she was probably right, but didn't have the practical skills to fix what turned out to be a minor medical issue. She told the crew to give him some orange juice and something to eat and sure enough, he was fine!

Once the "patient" was safely back in his seat and everything calmed down, we saw the crew bring a gift bottle of wine to the DOCTOR! Michelle essentially had the practical knowledge to take care of the emergency, but the doctor got the credit! I teased one of the flight attendants about it and once they realized Michelle had actually solved the problem, they gave her a bottle of wine as well.

The joke is, we had to change planes once we landed, and although we got the wine from a flight attendant on the same airline, they didn't allow us to bring it on the next flight! Who would you rather have take control of a situation like that? A surgeon who undoubtedly has more medical training to operate on patients, or a skilled nurse who has seen it all?

Many advisors, including me, are like the old skilled nurse. We know when to apply pressure to the wound, so to speak, and when to bandage it up. Financial designations are much the same. I know that when I run into a highly complex case, I may need to bring in other experts. I may consult with a CPA, or a tax attorney or an estate planning attorney. In fact, we consistently refer clients to other professionals when we know we need that additional expertise. For most of our clients, however, we are fully capable of handling their needs competently.

Ask about designations, but certainly, do not hang your selection process only that one thing. If someone wants a CFP, and they feel more comfortable with them, I am perfectly fine with that. You must decide if that's a deal breaker for you or not. In the GMTZ strategy, a designation is unnecessary to understand and implement the basic concepts involved. It requires knowledge of the use of life insurance as the base of your financial pyramid. We can build everything else on that solid foundation. If someone with a designation tells you this is unnecessary, I am interested in understanding a BETTER alternative. There are many ways to evaluate a new potential advisor, but here is a list of my top 10 questions to ask an advisor at your first meeting. I won't give you a list of acceptable answers. I simply counsel you to think of the responses to evaluate if you feel comfortable the advisor can help you Get to Zero.

1. What are your fundamental beliefs about money?

2. What is the most challenging financial problem you have had to solve for a client, and how did you do it?

3. What is the one financial problem you most commonly deal with when taking on a new client?

4. How do you hire staff and how long have they been here?

5. What tools do you use to analyze each new client's situation?

6. What do you believe about insurance products and risk transference?

7. If I met one of your clients on the golf course and your name or company came up in conversation, what is the first thing that person would likely say about you and your team?

8. What is most important to you when dealing with a new client?

9. Are there any financial "prejudices" you have, and if so, what are they?

10. What is going to be the number one benefit we receive from working with you and your firm?

You may ask how they get paid. You may also ask if they are a fiduciary by law and what that means. These are important questions, but they should disclose these WITHOUT you having to ask them. They may disclose it in firm brochures and other materials given to you.

Finally, and once again, if you're still here, I will assume you want to pursue a GMTZ strategy. If they don't ask about debt, but only about how much money you have and where it's invested, ask them what they believe about the three zeros! Here is a way to do so:

"Mr./Ms. Advisor, I just read a book called Get Me to Zero. It strongly suggested that the three most important financial goals to be achieved before retirement are 1) To have ZERO debt, including my home, 2) ZERO income taxes in retirement or as low of a tax liability and as close to zero as possible, and 3) ZERO risk in my draw-down assets in retirement. I have already concluded that this is where I want to go financially. What is your process to help me achieve those goals?"

You have read the book. Listen for the answers. If you need a second opinion or want someone else to look at what you are doing, we offer a second opinion service, which will afford you the chance to evaluate your decision on who to work with.

Hiring an advisor is like finding a money doctor. You don't need to be sick to go to your annual medical checkup, and neither does your financial house need to be sick to find an advisor. Once you realize that you're not feeling well, having a doctor is a good place to start. The same is true with a financial advisor. I like the word 'coach' much better. I believe it is my job to show you how to run certain financial "plays" to get you to zero, among other things. Find a coach you can trust. You will sleep better.

Chapter Ten

Never Trust a Skinny Chef!

Every Thursday night for the last several years, my wife Michelle and I have gone to a little Italian restaurant called Nonna Maria's Italian Kitchen, located less than 2 miles from our front door. It's exactly what you would expect from a great Italian place. Small, intimate, fabulous and I mean fabulous food, and after over two years of being Thursday night regulars, family! The owner, my friend Gerry and his crew, are some of the most wonderful people you would ever meet! If you are ever in the Albany, New York area, look it up! You won't be sorry!

Gerry and I talk all the time about how we try to fight off our aging by working out on a treadmill or, in my case, an elliptical machine every day. I know if Gerry stopped, just like if I stopped working out, we would be portly, or maybe, in my case, more portly than we are now. I love the saying not to trust a skinny cook. I always feel more confident following the advice of professionals who live what they preach.

Living what one preaches is not always easy, nor does the ideal always reflect the real. Why? Because life happens. Compounding variables raise their pernicious heads. The ideal, which I've outlined in the previous chapters, gets battered and bruised. Discouragement sometimes becomes an enemy to your ideal plans. But, remember, you are not crazy, you're just alive.

Permit me again to share how compounding variables, mostly out of my control, wreaked havoc on a perfect Get Me to Zero plan. Survival was only possible because financial foundations were securely in place. Thus, I will return to Zero.

My parents used to have an ashtray that said "Ve get too soon oldt, und too late Shmart." It's a little family heirloom that I keep nearby, not because I smoke, I don't, but because it reminds me of my mom and dad and a truism I never really understood until I reached my 60s.

In previous chapters, I've shared some of my shmart and not so shmart decisions. You will see how some shmart decisions may not be easy or financially prudent, but they are still right.

I am not debt free as I write this. I am, like you, returning to work on it.

Everyone has a life journey that is full of decisions that have a tremendous impact on your life in later years. I've thought about writing my life story, and I've shared it all with close friends, but I must tell you, I find myself in the same boat I'm writing about from time to time. For me, the pandemic changed everything about my focus. I won't get into the financial trouble we experienced when I tried to save my staff and kept paying them even though revenue fell dramatically. I am the fat cook. I am also like the old fat country doctor who tells you that you should lose weight. I am working on these issues in my current financial life. In 2019, even though my wife and I felt we were on solid financial footing and it looked like we were really sailing, both of our parents became terminally ill. We decided for Michelle to stop working and care for her dad. Michelle made a substantial income as a nurse mid-wife and women's health care nurse practitioner. We made the only decision we felt we could make, which was for Michelle to stop working to care for her father, we knew it would be difficult financially.

We lost about $100,000 per year of income and since I was on her health insurance; we had to pay $1,950 per month for COBRA. The following year, Covid-19 hit and not only did my practice take a massive hit to revenue, I, like many of you small business owners, tried to keep everyone employed.

I did not get into the retirement planning business to get wealthy. I left corporate employment because I wanted to row my own boat. I wanted to be free. I did not want a boss. Michelle's father eventually moved in with us, right before Covid hit. He never got it, thank God, but he died peacefully in our guest room with me holding his hand and Michelle lying next to him and hugging him. Having him live with us was one of the most difficult things we've ever done, but at the same time, it is also the most rewarding. We would do it again in a heartbeat.

I calculated the financial cost. Between the loss of Michelle's income, losing her ability to fund her 401(k), and the additional cost of health insurance and adding in a lost opportunity cost over our life expectancy, it came out to just over $650,000.

There is no price on love. We both loved Michelle's father very much.

Donald J. Deveau, her dad, died on October 29, 2020. Shortly after we laid him to rest near the town of Saugus, Massachusetts north of Boston, where he lived all his life, both Michelle and I came down with Covid. Right after we recovered, doctors diagnosed my 86-year-old mom with terminal cancer. She lived three hours away in Rhode Island. Though I have two siblings there, Michelle, who my mom loved dearly, wanted to do everything she could to take care of her. We went back and forth every weekend from early February all the way to her death on May 25th 2021. My beloved mother, Pauline M. Gallant, had a most profound impact on my life. I was fortunate enough to express this to her in a long letter when I learned of her diagnosis. Writing that letter to my mother, before she died, allowed me to express my thoughts in ways I could never have done in person. But she read it, and then we talked about it, laughed about it, and even cried about it. I know that it was as important to healing my grief as it was to her receiving it. Going back and forth to Rhode Island every weekend was exhausting emotionally and physically. All that time I was trying to run my business.

All of this opened my eyes to the number one priority I chose for my life since then, and that is to live each day to the fullest. I'm lucky that I'm married to my best friend. Michelle could qualify for Social Security Disability through all of this because, on top of dealing with caring for two sick parents, she has rheumatoid arthritis. In October 2022, we were both qualified to go on Medicare and we are no longer required to pay almost $2,000 per month for health care. So, I'm the fat cook. I have fresh debt issues as I write this, and implementing this strategy myself validates its effectiveness and value.

Because I'm not sitting on top of the debt-free mountain with rivers of money, I hesitated to write this book. What I've seen, what I've helped clients to do, and now experiencing its success myself, inspired this book. I wish I would have learned all about this a long time ago.

"Ve get too soon oldt, und too late Shmart."

But for anyone in life who is honest about life's experiences, you know we learn the hardest lessons from our decisions and consequences of those decisions. Morgan Housel's book really opened my eyes further. He talks about how Bill Gates was lucky enough to attend one of the few high schools in the world in Seattle that had a computer, and how that stroke of luck eventually gave us Microsoft. I highly recommend that you read his book. I have other recommended reading in the appendix.

I know for sure, because I can read, and I can deduce, that there are a lot of us hurting out there. Some statistics say that over 60% of the population can't cover a $5,000 surprise expense. Car repossessions are at an all-time high. People are being laid off all over the country as I write this in the Spring of 2023. Financial stress is one of the leading causes of divorce, substance abuse, and anxiety.

Now I have my mission. I am devoting the rest of my life to helping people get to zero. I am fortunate that I have great health, at least a good enough mind to finish this, my first book. Others will be coming. I have no plans to retire. Do not despair if you are in debt and it's causing you stress. There is a way out. Do not think that you don't have the power to arrange your financial life amazingly. You can. I hope this book helps you to do exactly that.

Final Thoughts

Thanks for joining me on this journey to help to get you to ZERO. I hope that you found the information in this book to be helpful, and hopefully it opened your eyes to a simple and straightforward way to plan for your retirement. I wanted to put a few things in perspective as a final thought.

Retirement is about much more than how you stand financially. This book has been all about how to get to Zero Debt, Zero Income Taxes, and Zero Risk in your draw-down assets once you retire. What is it about retirement that has so many financial advisors and Americans planning, talking, and thinking about this topic on a regular basis? I believe it has more to do with where we are at this golden age of our lives.

When I turned 60 about 5 and half years ago as I write this, I had this moment of clarity when I realized that the clock really is ticking on my time here on the planet! My wife, Michelle, also turned 60 the year I wrote this book and she and I have had many revelations about how our mind has shifted in terms of how we look at life. While I never plan to retire fully, Michelle, who is

retired, and I live a simple "retired lifestyle." In other words, we've found a few things that we are passionate about that we enjoy immensely at this time of our lives. One little treat we enjoy every Thursday is going to dinner at Nonna Maria's as I mentioned in Chapter 10. Depending upon whether we want to enjoy some wine with dinner, the cost is quite reasonable. More importantly, this little ritual has made us great friends! Here are a couple of pictures of us with the crew at Nonna's.

These folks help to brighten our day every Thursday evening. It's a simple pleasure, and it's the best kind! This is a family run business. Michelle and I were there when they opened again after the initial Covid-19 lock-down. There were only a few tables each night for many months as so many people were afraid to go out. We wanted to live our lives as normally as possible, and these friends helped us to do that! We decided to go ahead and enjoy the simple things and eating there without worrying about the virus was one of them. We're so glad we did.

I play golf on Friday mornings in a "Senior Men's Golf League." It's played at Bend of the River golf course in Hadley, NY (www. bendoftherivergc.com) which is a pretty, little golf course in the foothills of the Adirondack Mountains. About 60 to as many as 72 men, some of whom are well into their 80's show up every single Friday morning for an 8:30 am shotgun scramble. For non-golfers, that means everyone tees off around the same time on different holes in teams of four. It's a huge amount of fun, and the top prize might be three used balls (cleaned and shiny of course) for the winners. After the round, we have a couple of hot dogs, or a few slices of Pizza, and kibbitz about the missed putts and other tall tales of the day's round. But the important thing is, we have loads of fun. It costs $26.00 for 18 holes with riding cart!

I mention this because with both little weekly events, we get to enjoy the simplest things life has to offer, and for not a ton of money by a long shot. My buddies in the golf league have had wonderful careers with great life stories. Some have had fascinating careers. One friend was a tugboat captain. Another walked the beams to help build the first World Trade Center and he actually helped to pull the last survivor out of the rubble after 9-11. There are teachers, police officers, engineers, chefs, salesmen and more, and every week, I learn a little more about life just talking to these guys. I also have learned a ton about aging while having fun!

I don't know what your ultimate retirement goals might be. Maybe you want enough money to travel the world. Maybe you want a couple of vacation homes. Maybe your goal is to volunteer. Whatever it is, and I have countless clients and friends who will attest to this, make it simple. Find what your passion is and go out and live it! You can hike, bike, play tennis, pickle ball, horseshoes, quilt, read, walk, and learn, all for free. Retirement does not need to be expensive!

At my age it means much more to me, that we are one doctor's appointment away from our lives changing forever. That small pain that you know you should have checked out turns out to be something much more serious. You might have challenges caring for aging and ailing parents, which Michelle and I experienced in 2020 and 2021 with loss of her father, who lived with us for the last year of his life, and my mom who died 7 short months later. But through the caring process, we learned so much more about her dad and my mom and we would not change a thing, but it was part of this stage of our life.

I'm a huge believer that as humans we are given the gift of awareness. We are conscious of what we need to do each day and what is going on around us. As we age, we become more aware of the gifts we have each day, and we know that it is a time in life to be very grateful for what we have.

I'm not so naïve to believe that everyone needs to implement the Get Me to Zero strategy. There are wealthy individuals who actually use debt to create wealth. There are wealthy folks who have multiple assets that can be used in many creative ways to generate even more wealth. This book was not written for them. It was written for moms and dads who are out there working hard every day for a better life for themselves and their families. It was written for folks who are not likely to find themselves choosing which yacht to buy. It's for the folks who make this country run every day. You know if you're one of them or not. If you are, then this book is for you.

Enjoy your life every day. Become "Freetired" and gain financial confidence as quick as you can and believe that life still has wonderful simple pleasures to offer. My prayer is that you learn this lesson sooner than later as you go on your journey to Zero!

Appendix
Recommended Reading

The Psychology of Money
by Morgan Housel

The Pirates of Manhattan I and II
by Barry James Dyke

Guaranteed Income
by Barry James Dyke

The Power of Zero
by David McKnight

Look Before You LIRP
by David McKnight

SMART Retirement
by Matt Zagula

How Privatized Banking Really Works
by L. Carlos Lara and Robert P. Murphy Ph. D.

www.ingramcontent.com/pod-product-compliance
Lightning Source LLC
Chambersburg PA
CBHW040755220326
41597CB00029BB/4921